WOMEN
KNOW
CYBER

100 Fascinating Females
Fighting Cybercrime

WOMEN
KNOW
CYBER

100 Fascinating Females
Fighting Cybercrime

STEVE MORGAN & DI FREEZE

WOMEN KNOW CYBER: 100 Fascinating Females
Fighting Cybercrime

Cybersecurity Ventures
83 Main Street, 2nd Floor, Suite 5
Northport, N.Y. 11768

This book is dedicated to my six children. Without you, my first book would have been completed thirty years ago.

I thank God for showing me what's most important in life.

– Steve Morgan

Cybersecurity Conference Sponsor

FutureCon produces cutting-edge events aimed at CISOs, IT security professionals, and cybersecurity companies – bringing together the best minds in the industry for a unique experience. These one-day events in more than 20 cities throughout North America feature thought-provoking presentations by industry leaders, esteemed keynote speakers, and a panel session with cybersecurity experts.

Each FutureCon event provides attendees with the very latest and highest level vendor-neutral training in the security community. FutureCon's founder, Kim Hakim, is a U.S. Navy veteran with more than two decades of experience producing thousands of cybersecurity conferences.

"Women Know Cyber" book signings and special programs will be held at FutureCon events.

https://FutureconEvents.com/

twitter.com/futurecon2019

Contents

Foreword

– Sylvia Acevedo is a well-known author, entrepreneur, engineer, and rocket scientist.

The trailblazing women featured in this book represent the best of what our collective action against cybercrime can be. They have committed themselves to the mission of keeping our country safe from those who would do us harm and are on the front lines every day fighting everything from extortion and theft to espionage and data manipulation.

Cybersecurity is everyone's problem. Cyber threats are hitting people with greater regularity, they will continue, and they will metastasize. National security and personal security vulnerabilities are at an all-time high.

But when you look at the cybersecurity industry, women make up only 20 percent of the workforce. So we have to ask ourselves: if cybersecurity is everyone's problem, why isn't a greater cross-section of society solving it? Why aren't there more women like the 100 featured here?

This represents a real vulnerability for our

country, because if we have half of the population that is largely left out of the national fight against hacks, identity theft, malware, data breaches, and other cybersecurity battlegrounds, imagine the strategic and tactical blind spots we allow to take root.

As the world is being rewritten line by line and recreated around data every day, it's critical that more women are at the table making decisions and contributing to our lines of defense. Inclusion is not just an HR buzzword — in our multicultural, dynamic, and ever-changing society, it is an absolute national imperative that we have a diversity of input and perspective when developing cybersecurity tools.

The more perspectives we have, the fewer blind spots and unknown unknowns there are — and the quicker corrections can be made.

I'm so inspired by these pioneering women and encouraged by their stories. Because of out-of-the-box thinkers, innovators, and leaders like them, the fight against cybercrime is entering a new era where women are confidently adding their voices to the mix — not just creating a path for themselves, but opening up opportunities for others forging ahead in their wake.

The safety and security of our country depends upon more women raising their hand and engaging in this fight. I hope this book shows that they are welcome at the table. Thank you to Steve Morgan for compiling this book of female cyber leaders.

– Sylvia Acevedo is an award-winning entrepreneur who has earned worldwide recognition for her work in addressing one of society's most vexing challenges — universal access to education.

Sylvia started her career as a rocket scientist at the Jet Propulsion Labs where she worked on the Voyager mission's fly by of Jupiter and its moons and the Solar Polar/Probe missions.

As an engineer at IBM, she led the redesign of state-of-the-art manufacturing facilities that became an international showcase. Leveraging her technical training in the technology industry, she served as an executive with Fortune 100 companies: Apple, Autodesk and Dell. She holds a master's degree in Systems Engineering from Stanford University where she was one of the first Hispanics, male or female, to have earned a graduate engineering degree. Sylvia earned her bachelor's degree in Industrial Engineering from New Mexico State University, which in 2010, named Sylvia as one of their most Distinguished Engineering Alumni.

twitter.com/SylviaAcevedo
linkedin.com/in/sylviaacevedo1/
https://sylviaacevedo.org/

Preface

@WomenKnowCyber is a social media movement for females fighting cybercrime.

On a warm summer afternoon in late June 2018, the editor-in-chief (@CybersecuritySF) at Cybercrime Magazine, which is published by Cybersecurity Ventures, shouted out an idea to everyone in our office: "Let's start up a list of women in cybersecurity."

What good reason is there to create a list of women in cybersecurity, let alone what's the best way to research and publish it? Before we could ask ourselves that question, the first responder, Casey Morgan, a 16-year-old (now 17) summer intern, and our youngest woman in cyber, swiveled around in her chair and said, "OK, I'll do it." The rest of our small team (made up of more women than men) chimed in with an enthusiastic "Yes!" — and we were off to the races.

For better or worse — and without giving it more than a few minutes of thought — Twitter was the starting point. Casey's older sister, Kerry Morgan, a 21-year-old (now 22) full-time employee and our special projects and operations manager, volunteered to be the social media coach.

The two girls dove headfirst into the project with a youthful enthusiasm that immediately bore results. After a full day of researching the names of women in cybersecurity on Twitter, Casey produced nearly 100 of them. Our editorial filter brought that number down to 58. We were after as many women in cyber as we could find — including coders, ethical hackers, CISOs and IT security leaders, cyber forensics experts, specialized journalists covering the field, and others — but we didn't want names just for the sake of saying we had lots of them.

On June 26, 2018, we posted a blog on Cybercrime Magazine, "58 Women In Cybersecurity To Follow On Twitter, And More Names On The Way," and then tweeted it out and shared it on LinkedIn. Dozens of women (and some men) sent us messages about the list. To paraphrase what they said, in a nutshell, is "Thanks for the list" and "here's some names of women in cybersecurity for you to add." Some people volunteered the Twitter handles for one or two colleagues, and others provided us with dozens of contacts.

Casey worked diligently on researching names for us over the summer — even during her vacation time in Vermont and elsewhere when she'd pop open her laptop to squeeze in an extra hour here or there. As she went along, Cybercrime Magazine posted a weekly blog with the latest tally of names — 132, 181, 247, 345, and so on — until we hit around 1,000 names and Casey returned to high school for her junior year. We owe her a debt of gratitude for compiling the initial list. She came up with processes for consulting our staff on quality control, reviewing external submissions, avoiding duplicates, and finding new names.

After the first 90 days or so of compilation, the top FAQ we had from Cybercrime Magazine's readers and Cybersecurity Ventures' followers was, "Why don't you take the names and turn them into a Twitter list so we can follow it?" Our answer — that makes perfect sense. That would also bring the benefit of auto-updating profiles when people change jobs, and building a social community movement aimed at generating more awareness around women in our industry.

In the fall of 2018, our managing editor, Di Freeze, got involved with the project. She helped prepare us for the move to a Twitter list, and on Oct. 31, 2018, Cybercrime Magazine launched the @WomenKnowCyber Twitter account. Di then set about curating a Twitter list by going back through the first 1,000+ names we compiled — and adding them to the new list dubbed "Women In Cybersecurity 1" (Twitter currently limits lists to 5,000 contacts and we are planning multiple lists).

Di's curation is a healthy mix of social media and editorial. She uses a standard format to provide followers with one tweet containing 5 new names every day (Monday through

Saturday, and a day off on Sunday), including their Twitter handle and a short description. Di personally selects five interesting women for each tweet — and there's no other tweets on the account.

After @WomenKnowCyber was up and running, we posted a new blog on Cybercrime Magazine — which has our Women In Cybersecurity list embedded as part of our editorial. It's a great way for our readers to keep up on the list in real time and to read Di's curation in a larger format that is easy on the eyes.

@WomenKnowCyber doesn't follow anyone on Twitter except for a handful of our staff. And yet, we have more than 1,000 followers on the still relatively new account. These are mainly high-quality followers from the technology and cybersecurity fields. The Retweet and Like activity is high (in proportion to the number of followers) most every day, and hardly a complaint (there was one). Most importantly, the praise and thanks we've received for the list have been loud and continuous. These pretty good stats tell us that there's a lot of community interest in our list.

Going forward, we are committed to building up the @WomenKnowCyber list, and the daily tweet, as an important part of our editorial and community development. Cybercrime Magazine has met some incredible people directly through the Twitter account — which has led to interviews, stories, and podcasts on our media.

That sums up the history of our women in cybersecurity list. We are hoping that one day it will go down in history as what one woman described to us on the phone as "a social media movement for females fighting cybercrime."

If nothing else, the @WomenKnowCyber list has become part of a new roll call of women in cybersecurity — which is recalculating the number of women represented in our field from 11 percent based on a six-year-old survey which states the needle hasn't moved one iota in all that time ... to 20 percent in 2019. Interestingly, many highly accomplished women on our list — including some with outstanding IT security skills — would not qualify to be counted as women in cybersecurity based on the criteria used by the old survey.

A quick "Thanks!" to the dozens of women (and some men) — you know who you are — who have taken the time to give us direct feedback on our original list and subsequent @WomenKnowCyber list. Without you, the list would not be what it is. We also appreciate the names that you've shared with us.

All of the women, of course, were found on the @WomenKnowCyber list.

Women In Cybersecurity

Cyber has a gender problem, if our industry continues to regurgitate numbers from a six-year-old report that states an alarmingly low percentage of women hold security positions.

Research firm Frost and Sullivan authored a report in 2013, which states that women make up 11 percent of the global cybersecurity workforce. The report is co-branded with (ISC)2 foundation, now a part of The Center for Cyber Safety and Education, and widely circulated in the media.

In the absence of any new research data published by another source, the 11 percent figure continues to show up in the media — despite a substantial rise in the number of women in the cybersecurity field — perpetuating the stigma of too few women in cybersecurity.

Research from Cybersecurity Ventures, which first appeared in the media early last year, predicts that women will represent more than 20 percent of the global cybersecurity workforce by the end of 2019. This is based on in-depth discussions with numerous industry experts in cybersecurity and human talent, vetting, analyzing and synthesizing third-party reports, surveys, and media sources, and conducting our own list compilation.

The 20 percent figure is still way too low, and our industry needs to continue pushing for more women in cyber. But, heightened awareness on the topic — led by numerous women in cyber associations and initiatives — has helped move the needle in a positive direction.

We are recalculating the number of women in cyber based on a broader definition of positions covered. We've evolved the roll call from traditional "IT security (aka Information security)" titles found mainly in mid-sized to large organizations, to the "cybersecurity" roles in a much larger and fast-growing industry.

"I started out often being the only woman in the room — and now I'm seeing not only more women in the room, but also women of color. That makes me happy on so many levels," says Rosa Smothers, SVP of Cyber Operations at KnowBe4, a top security awareness and phishing simulation vendor.

Smothers took a path different from most people to the upper echelons of cybersecurity. She started out as a sales engineer — and then was a technical intelligence officer at the CIA for over a decade, also doing a rotation at the NSA. The benefit of solving problems with diverse perspectives was a lesson she learned at the CIA, and she's happy to have this same experience in her role at KnowBe4.

IT security is in fact a subset of cybersecurity. Cybersecurity Ventures looks beyond securing

100 Fascinating Females Fighting Cybercrime

corporate networks (which has seen a rise in the number of women), and includes IoT security, IIoT and ICS security, medical device security, automotive cybersecurity, aviation cybersecurity, military cyber defense technology, and others. Further, we cover the cybersecurity service provider ecosystem, which also includes women-owned small businesses, and broadens to include digital forensics and other jobs.

We include Israel, the world's second-largest exporter of cyber technology (behind the U.S.), which bolsters an impressive and growing head count of female cybersecurity founders and professionals. In 2018, TechCrunch reported that for the most recent year tracked, 15 percent of newly established Israeli cybersecurity startups had a female founder, an increase from 5 percent the previous year.

Women are participating in Australia's cybersecurity workforce at much higher rates than the purported 11 percent global figure. The 2018 McAfee Cybersecurity Talent Study states that Australia's cybersecurity workforce is 25 percent female.

According to industry body National Association of Software and Services Companies, the strength of the women workforce in the information technology and services industry in India currently stands at 34 percent. "There is certainly a rising trend among women to take up the cybersecurity domain for their profession," stated Jamuna Swamy, an award-winning CISO based in India. Last year, Microsoft India and Data Security Council of India (DSCI) launched CyberShikshaa, a three-year program to create a pool of skilled cybersecurity women professionals in the country.

BeecherMadden, a leading, award-winning U.K. and U.S. cybersecurity recruitment business, conducted research which showed that the U.K. cybersecurity industry is now 18 percent female. "Given that increasing the number of women in cybersecurity is a goal that many companies hold, we should all be pleased that we have started making progress," states Karla Reffold, COO and founder of BeecherMadden. "18 percent still doesn't go far enough, and while 50 percent may seem far away, there are some companies at this level already."

Cybersecurity Ventures isn't the only research firm noticing an uptick of women in cybersecurity. Forrester Research analyst Stephanie Balaouras, who co-authored a recent report with fellow analyst Claire O'Malley, told Dark Reading that she believes women now represent somewhere between 15-20 percent of the industry if you include security and risk, privacy, and compliance and audit functions.

Forrester also predicts that the number of women CISOs at Fortune 500 companies will rise to 20 percent in 2019, compared with 13 percent in 2017. This is consistent with new research from Boardroom Insiders which states that 20 percent of Fortune 500 global chief information officers (CIOs) are now women — the largest percentage ever.

In a survey of 300 women that were employed in cybersecurity, less than 50 percent of the respondents said that they had entered the field via IT or Computer Science. The respondents are diverse in their backgrounds, coming from Compliance, Psychology, Internal Audit, Entrepreneurship, Sales, Art, and more. The pipeline of women entering the cybersecurity field is as far and wide as employers are willing to imagine.

An old school accounting of women in cybersecurity focuses mainly on "corporate IT security" and excludes (or substantially limits) startups and companies with less than 500 employees; large swaths of risk, compliance and privacy; and other roles, and concludes that women are barely represented in cyber — sending the wrong message to young girls that may be open to pursuing an education and future career in our field. It's time to go new school on this topic — and send out a new and accurate message about the number of women in cybersecurity.

"You know what, I see the change firsthand," says Robert Herjavec, founder and CEO of Herjavec Group, a $300 million cybersecurity company with offices in the U.S., Canada, and Europe. "The number of women I meet every day in our industry has gone way up — not to mention in the boardroom and technical, high-level positions. And I have to say — as a 'Cyber CEO,' it's great to see organizations actively working towards this change."

Amy Hess, executive assistant director (EAD) of the Criminal, Cyber, Response and Services Branch at the Federal Bureau of Investigation (FBI), and Tonya Ugoretz, deputy assistant director of the FBI's Cyber Division, are the first women to occupy their respective posts — in a field, and agency — that has been dominated by men, according to an article in The Wall Street Journal.

"Over time what I've seen is that it's helpful for young women and girls in school to see somebody that looks like them in these (cybersecurity) spots," Hess told Cybercrime Magazine in an interview at FBI headquarters in Washington, D.C. recently. "That's something that I've grown to appreciate more and more so in the past several years — to say and to see that you can achieve this too, I'm no different than any of them."

"My company employs 42 people (and growing), 40 percent of them women," says

Theresa Payton, CEO at Fortalice Solutions and the former White House CIO. "Also, fraud prevention and cybersecurity are now converging. And there are a lot of women who are in fraud operations — which was previously paper-based and is now digital — who can come work in cybersecurity."

Payton, a visible spokesperson for the industry and the founder of a fledgling cybersecurity company, and the women working for her, would not count in the old 11 percent report. They aren't employed by mid-sized or large corporations, and they aren't coders — despite the fact that they are highly accomplished cyber fighters.

"When I first started hosting cybersecurity conferences (more than a decade ago) it was very rare, maybe out of the audience you'd have two or three women; now I'd say sometimes almost half the audience, maybe not quite half, but almost," says Kim Hakim, a U.S. Navy veteran and founder of FutureCon, which produces events in 24 North American cities this year. "It's great to see all the women that are now in the industry and it's a great career for all of our daughters. The limits are endless. I mean, you can go very far in this industry."

"I am seeing more women attending conferences now than ever before," adds Payton. "And I don't mean all women conferences where the events were based around discussing ways to fight the unfair balance of men and women in the cybersecurity space. I see a lot more women at the big cyber conferences. There are a lot more women involved than ever before."

The RSA Conference USA 2019 held recently in San Francisco — which is the world's largest cybersecurity event with more than 42,000 people and 740 speakers — is another measuring stick for representation of women in our field. "At this year's conference, 46 percent of all keynote speakers were women," according to Sandra Toms, VP and curator, RSA Conference, in a blog she posted on the last day of this year's event. "While RSAC keynotes saw near gender parity this year, women made up 32 percent of our overall speakers," noted Toms.

Cybercrime will more than triple the number of job openings over the next five years. Cybersecurity Ventures predicts there will be 3.5 million cybersecurity job openings by 2021. To fill the world's open security positions, we'll need to aim for 50 percent of women in cyber over the next decade. While some people may view that as an overly ambitious goal, it's one that the cybersecurity industry must aim for.

"Cybersecurity is one of the only professions that has almost every job within it," says Shamla Naidoo, global CISO at IBM. Naidoo says that you can be an engineer, a communications person, or a developer, and find your place in the cybersecurity field. She points out opportunities for women to write policy, get involved with corporate governance, or to do hard-core forensics.

Cybersecurity Ventures concurs with Naidoo. Our @WomenKnowCyber list contains thousands of women in cybersecurity — many of them with strong cybersecurity technical skills and yet would not qualify to be counted into the old 11 percent survey.

Can we all agree to disagree with the notion that the cybersecurity field hasn't made any progress over the past six years and we're still stuck at 11 percent of women in cybersecurity — when there are so many experienced experts, analysts and data pointing to more female representation than ever before?

Steve Morgan is founder and editor-in-chief at Cybersecurity Ventures.

Reprinted with permission from Cybercrime Magazine. Read the full report at: https://WomenInCyber.com

Introduction

 Women know cyberse-curity and they're heavily involved in our industry. Don't let anyone or any survey tell you otherwise. Just in case you don't believe it, we've written a book to help prove it. It's a new wave book that is based on the Twitter list @WomenKnowCyber researched and compiled by Cybercrime Magazine and published by Cybersecurity Ventures.

"Women Know Cyber: 100 Fascinating Females Fighting Cybercrime" features cybersecurity experts from across the globe, with varying backgrounds, who stand out for protecting governments, businesses, and people from cybercrime — and for their contributions to our community.

If these 100 leading ladies aren't proof enough for you, then we encourage you to look at the @WomenKnowCyber Twitter list. You'll see thousands of women in cybersecurity — from coders to digital forensics experts to chief information security officers at the world's largest corporations. The list grows larger every day.

Are women underrepresented in cybersecurity? Yes. Cybersecurity Ventures predicts that women will hold approximately 20 percent of the positions in our field by the end of this year. But, that is up from an 11 percent figure which has been circulating for the past six years. Make no mistake about it — women are trending up in cybersecurity.

How do we move the needle from 20 percent to 50 percent in the coming years? One answer may be that we need to look at the glass as being half-full, rather than half-empty — as has been the case for way too long by way too many people. Let's highlight the sheer number of women in cybersecurity — in an effort to attract more women to an industry that desperately needs them.

Cybersecurity Ventures predicts that there will be 3.5 million unfilled cybersecurity jobs globally by 2021, up from 1 million positions in 2014. The job openings are driven by a huge increase in cybercrime, which is predicted to cost the world $6 trillion annually by 2021, up from $3 trillion in 2015.

There's a cybersecurity career waiting for every girl and woman that wants one and is willing to gain the skills needed for employment. We hope that this book will inspire you — or someone you know — to think about becoming a woman in cybersecurity.

Steve Morgan is founder and editor-in-chief at Cybersecurity Ventures

Permissions and Safety

Although the 100 fascinating females fighting cybercrime have public profiles on Twitter (and other social media), the publisher and co-authors of "Women Know Cyber" have been granted permission by each person to include their name, photo, and curated biographical information in this book.

We provide a Twitter account name for each person in the book. Where publicly available, we provide additional social media account names and websites.

Twitter is committed to making its social media a safe place for free expression. Twitter's dedication and approach to safety and security is important to us — because we aim to reach students, parents, educators, and all of society with this book. To learn more about safety on Twitter, go here:
https://about.twitter.com/en_us/safety.html

Many of the profiles in this book contain LinkedIn profiles. LinkedIn too, is committed to providing safe connections between its members. To learn more about safety on LinkedIn, go here:
https://safety.linkedin.com/

I am woman, hear me roar
In numbers too big to ignore

Helen Reddy / Ray Burton

Alissa (Dr. Jay) Abdullah
@dralissajay

Dr. A Abdullah (Johnson) ~ Fortune 100 #CISO ~ Fmr Deputy CIO @WhiteHouse #44 ~ Huff Post Top 100 Social CIOs ~ My thoughts are my own. ~ Will work for shoes

Alissa (aka Dr. Jay) Abdullah, Ph.D., is chief information security officer (CISO) for Xerox and former deputy chief information officer (CIO) for the White House.

This F100 executive has been involved with security for more than 25 years. She started out in her career as a cryptologic engineer with the U.S. Department of Defense (DoD), serving as a mathematician, electrical engineer, and project manager for a myriad of cryptographic systems. In her role as deputy CIO for the White House, she oversaw the White House information technology infrastructure and budget, including EOP government and contractor staff across multiple data centers and remote locations.

She was deputy CTO for Lockheed Martin IT. As the first CISO of Stryker, she led and managed information security initiatives globally and worked closely with the different business leaders and regional infrastructure heads to ensure security policy or strategy was implemented in a consistent way. She is also the CISO Ambassador for Cybersecurity Ventures.

She was named to Black Enterprise's Most Powerful Women in Corporate America list in 2019 and Most Powerful Executives in Corporate America in 2017, and to HuffPost's Top 100 Most Social CIOs in 2015 and 2016.

linkedin.com/in/dralissajay/

Lillian Ablon
@LilyAblon

Security, Threat & Vulnerability for Internet of Things @Ring/@Amazon; Women in STEM; Social Engineering (#SECTF DEFCON Black Badge). @ RANDCorporation alumna.

Lillian Ablon is an information scientist and cybersecurity and emerging technology strategist. She is also a DEF CON "Uber" Black Badge recipient, a professor, a congressional expert witness, and a trusted expert for news outlets including The Washington Post, CNN, Bloomberg, CBS, NPR, The New York Times, Wired, TechCrunch, and the Los Angeles Times.

She has 14 years of experience creating and working with cutting edge technology and developing solutions for policy makers. Her research focus has been on computer/cybersecurity, security standards, the data breach ecosystem, deep and dark web, and the human element in cybersecurity.

Lillian is currently senior security technical program manager at Amazon and at Ring. She conducted research for the RAND Corporation for more than seven years. Prior to joining RAND, she worked at the Department of Defense, creating some of the most cutting edge technologies in cryptography, network exploitation and vulnerability analysis, and mathematics.

She holds a B.A. in pure mathematics from the University of California, Berkeley, and an M.S. in applied and computational mathematics from Johns Hopkins University.

linkedin.com/in/ablon/

Heather Adkins
@argvee

Director, Security & Privacy @Google My views are my own. I want to be a medieval historian when I grow up. She/Her.

Heather Adkins is a 17-year Google veteran and founding member of the Google Security Team. As senior director of Information Security and Privacy, she has built a global team responsible for maintaining the safety and security of Google's networks, systems, and applications.

Heather has an extensive background in systems and network administration with an emphasis on practical security. She has worked to build and secure some of the world's largest infrastructure.

Over her long career, she has tackled issues from a variety of domains including information security, insider threats, and privacy. This has included working high-profile incidents seen in the headlines every day that affect millions of people, such as Operation Aurora and the 2016 U.S. election.

Heather now focuses her time primarily on the defense of Google's computing infrastructure and working with industry to tackle some of the greatest security challenges as part of the Defending Digital Democracy project at the Belfer Center for Science and International Affairs at Harvard Kennedy School.

linkedin.com/in/argvee/
Heather Adkins photo courtesy Brandon Downey

Parry Aftab
@parryaftab

Digital Privacy & Cybersecurity Lawyer. Founder StopCyberbullying, WiredSafety, WiredTrust, & Cybersafety India, Author, Keynote Speaker and Advisor

Parry Aftab is managing director of Wire-Trust. She was among the world's first cyber-lawyers and was the founder of the first cybersafety and help group more than 23 years ago. Since then, she has been on the front line protecting children, families, vulnerable communities, and consumers.

As a digital privacy and security lawyer, she has advised nations, UNESCO, and the UN, digital and entertainment industry leaders, and well-known household brands. She has been named to and headed national and global task forces.

Parry is a sought-after expert and advisor whose unique insight into social media risks and how to design approaches, policies, and procedures to address them is among the most respected in the world. She is an award-winning columnist and author of several books on cybersafety. She has also contributed to several books on cyberlaw, life skills, and child sexual abuse.

Children are her passion, and protecting them her priority, so it's no wonder she is often called "The Kids Internet Lawyer." She helped design Singapore's cybersafety program, Girl Scouts' cybersafety program, and MTV's athinline.org. Marvel featured her in a Spider-Man comic on cyberbullying.

linkedin.com/in/parryaftab/
aftab.com

Dr. Mary Aiken
@maryCyPsy

Cyberpsychologist | Global Fellow Wilson Center | Writer | Speaker | Broadcaster | Advisor |

Dr. Mary Aiken is a cyberpsychologist, an academic advisor to Europol's European Cyber Crime Centre (EC3), and a member of the EC3 Advisory Group. She has advised at national and European levels in policy debates at the intersection of technology and human behavior and has published and spoken internationally on this topic.

Her work inspired the CBS series, "CSI: Cyber." Her book, "The Cyber Effect," was a 2016 Times Book of the Year in the Thought Category and 2016 Best Science Pick by Nature Int. Journal. She was inducted into the Infosecurity Europe Hall of Fame in 2017 in recognition of her contribution to the information and cybersecurity sector.

Dr. Aiken is a global fellow at the Washington DC Wilson Center and a fellow of the Society for Chartered IT Professionals. She has served as an adjunct associate professor at University College Dublin and Geary Institute for Public Policy, and as a distinguished professor of the Practice of Cyber Analytics at AIRS and sense-making fellow at the IBM Network Science Research Centre. She is the former director of the Royal College of Surgeons Cyberpsychology Research Centre.

linkedin.com/in/
professor-mary-aiken-149a106/

Baan Alsinawi
@talatek

TalaTek is a woman-owned business providing specialized services in risk management, security and compliance. Talk to us. We're problem solvers.#DigitalTransformation

Baan Alsinawi is the founder, president, and CEO of TalaTek, an integrated risk management firm. Her vision for TalaTek, which she started in 2006, was the need for an integrated platform that could both control security and minimize risk, and which could be implemented to ensure compliance by agencies and organizations.

Baan is a thought leader who sees the big picture, understands how technology can be leveraged, and knows how to build the right teams and solutions to manage it.

She is a member of (ISC)2 and is CISSP and ITIL certified. She has more than two decades of experience in information technology and has served in various capacities from managing networks and software sales to directing security operations.

Previously, Baan served as security director of IntelliDyne and a sales engineer at McAfee and Nortel. She began her career with EDS as a systems and network engineer.

linkedin.com/in/baanalsinawi/

Christina Ayiotis
@christinayiotis

#CyberStrategist #MotherOfMathGoddess
#Cook #WorldTraveller #InfoSec
#InfoGov #Privacy #SocialMedia
#CyberRiskManagement
#DigitalTransformation

Christina Ayiotis is a cyber strategist who provides strategic and operational consulting regarding cyber risk management and preparedness, incident/breach response, information governance, data privacy, government and internal investigations, e-discovery, records and information management, ethics, and emerging technology/innovation.

She is an independent consultant who recently served as chief cybersecurity officer of WiseLaw. She was a member of the adjunct facility, Department of Computer Science, George Washington University, for seven years.

Solutions Review recognized Christina as one of the Top 15 Women in Cybersecurity and InfoSec Today in 2019. She was ranked #18 on Thomson Reuters' 2018 List of Top 50 Social Influencers in Risk, Compliance and RegTech.

In the last decade, she has met thousands of people through her extensive volunteer work, as well as attendance at hundreds of events as a speaker/organizer or attendee.

linkedin.com/in/
christinaayiotiscyberattorney/

Debra Baker
@deb_infosec

CISSP CCSP Cybersecurity Evangelist Contributor to The Language of #CyberSecurity book. Tweets are my own. https://debinfosec.com

Debra Baker is a principal security engineer at Cygnacom Solutions. In that role and as a public key infrastructure and identity and access management expert, she conducts security audits, writes PKI CP/CPS, and consults on securing the blockchain.

With over 20 years of experience in the IT security field, she has broad experience in information security and risk, cryptography, network security, application security, operations security, and compliance. She worked at Cisco for seven years, including positions as product compliance engineer and regulatory compliance manager.

She was principal security engineer for Corsec Security, senior common criteria evaluator for Entrust's Cygnacom Solutions Division, and senior security engineer for Entrust. She also served as a network management integrator for IBM and communications specialist for the U.S. Air Force.

Debra is a co-founder of the League of Women in Cybersecurity and the founder of the Johns Hopkins University Cryptographic Knowledge Base - CryptoDoneRight.

linkedin.com/in/debrabakernc/

Ann Barron-DiCamillo
@annie_bdc

15+yrs #CyberSecurityOps taught me no target remains static; no offensive / defense capability is indefinitely effective; & NO advantage is permanent = my opinions

Ann Barron-DiCamillo is VP, Cyber Threat Intelligence and Incident Response at American Express. She is responsible for managing global cybersecurity operations and directing cyber threat intelligence, information security monitoring, and security incident response.

She was previously director of the United States Computer Emergency Readiness Team (US-CERT) at the Department of Homeland Security.

A recognized cybersecurity expert, Ann was named Top 50 Cyber Influencer of 2018 by CyberScoop, and in the same year, Top 10 Women in Cybersecurity by CyberDB and Top 15 Women in Cybersecurity by InfoSec. In 2017, CyberScoop named her the Top Woman in Cybersecurity, Incapsula selected her as part of their Top 50 Women in Internet Security, and Reciprocity named her to the list of InfoSec Experts You Should Follow On Twitter Right Now.

Past recognition includes Top 10 Women Power Players in IT Security by SC Magazine and Top 10 Women Cyber Guardians You Should Know by Nextgov.

linkedin.com/in/
ann-barron-dicamillo-46286b50/

Nicole Beckwith
@NicoleBeckwith

PCAPs make me happy. OSINT is my jam. Sr. Cyber Intel Analyst. Former DFIR & Investigator for State & Feds. Speaker. Shark Diver. Sniper.

Nicole Beckwith is a senior cyber intelligence analyst for GE Aviation.

She is a former state police officer and federally sworn U.S. marshal. She worked as a fraud investigator and digital forensic examiner for the state of Ohio and a task force officer for the United States Secret Service in their Financial and Electronic Crimes division. She is an international speaker recognized in the field of information security, policy, and cybercrime.

Nicole was trained by the United States Secret Service at the National Computer Forensics Institute in digital forensics, network investigations, network intrusion response, and virtual currency investigations. She has worked with numerous local, state, and federal law enforcement partners on criminal investigations including the FBI's Public Corruption Unit and Homeland Security Investigations.

She recently developed two cybersecurity training programs, teaching more than 1,600 officers how to respond to cybercrime and over 4,400 government employees on information security best practices.

linkedin.com/in/
nicole-beckwith-2ba87b166/

Puneet Bhasin
@cyberlawpuneet

Cyber Law Expert. Author. Speaker. Specialising in Cyber crime cases, E-commerce legal compliance, Block chain laws, IoT laws, AI laws, Cyber forensic laws.

Advocate Puneet Bhasin is a pioneer in technology laws in India and a cyber law expert practicing in Mumbai in matters involving cyber crimes, e-commerce, and intellectual property disputes in cyber space.

She is the founder of Cyberjure Legal Consulting, a Mumbai based firm specializing in technology, media, and entertainment laws. Her clients include nationalized banks, multi-national corporations and companies for cyber crime cases, along with information technology law audits, GDPR compliance audits, and cybersecurity audits.

Puneet is a pioneer of blockchain laws in India and the only advocate practicing in smart contracts legal compliance and legal compliance of blockchain applications. She is an advisor to the Rajya Sabha Committee on formulation of Internet and technology laws in India.

She is also a member of the Cyber Security Task Force Working Group, an initiative by Data Security Council of India in collaboration with NASSCOM.

linkedin.com/in/
advpuneetbhasincyberlawyer/

Justine Bone
@justinembone

#healthcare #hacking #hashtags: #cybersecurity in heels

Justine Bone is currently CEO at MedSec, a cybersecurity research company formed exclusively to serve the health care industry. Her previous roles include CISO at Dow Jones, global head of risk management at Bloomberg, and CEO of Immunity Inc. (now Cyxtera).

Justine began her career as a vulnerability researcher with Internet Security Systems (now IBM) X-Force and New Zealand's Government Communications Security Bureau. She has successfully launched, grown, and pivoted solutions within several companies, introducing new solutions and enabling competitive differentiation while building high quality and resilient systems.

As a member of HP's Security Advisory Board, chairperson of Miami Children Corp, an invited member of the Black Hat USA guest review board, and advisor to several technology companies, she leans on her background in vulnerability research and business leadership to advise a diverse set of interests.

Justine also enjoys remaining closely involved with the hacker community as organizer of the cybersecurity industry's Pwnie Awards.

linkedin.com/in/justinebone/

Eileen Brewer
@totheleftieileen

**Director @Symantec | Professional Mentor
@TechWomen | Investor @GoldenSeeds |
Speaker, panelist, workshop leader | World
Wonderer**

Eileen Brewer is a speaker, panelist, and workshop leader focused on empowering women and girls globally.

She has worked in the tech industry for 20 years. Her current position is as a director at Symantec. She oversees the Symantec security appliance business, from hardware product development through global supply chain.

Symantec is a host company for the U.S. State Department TechWomen Program where Eileen has volunteered as a professional mentor since 2012. Eileen hosts women from the Middle East, Africa, and Central Asia and facilitates technical and leadership training. She travels to these regions on delegation trips and through her own grassroots efforts to reach women in countries where the State Department has not officially organized trips.

In her passion to help advance the status of women and girls, she has developed speaking topics, panels, and workshops. She is tireless at learning, creating content, and sharing information with others to help them succeed.

Eileen is also managing director (investor role) at Golden Seeds, a group of investors seeking and funding high-potential, women-led businesses.

linkedin.com/in/eileenbrewer/

Julie Brill
@JulieSBrill

@Microsoft Corporate VP & Deputy GC for Global Privacy & Regulatory Affairs, Former Commissioner of US Federal Trade Commission, mom, wife.

Julie Brill is corporate VP and deputy general counsel for Global Privacy and Regulatory Affairs at Microsoft.

She was previously a partner at Hogan Lovells and co-director of the firm's privacy and cybersecurity practice. She served as a commissioner of the Federal Trade Commission from April 2010 to March 2016.

Prior to that role, she served as an assistant attorney general for Consumer Protection and Antitrust for the State of Vermont for over 20 years. She also was a lecturer-in-law at Columbia University's School of Law. She clerked for Vermont Federal District Court Judge Franklin S. Billings Jr.

Julie has received numerous national awards for her work, including the International Association of Privacy Professionals Privacy Leader of the Year Award and the New York University School of Law Alumna of the Year Award. National Law Journal named her a Cybersecurity Trailblazer in 2017. She was elected to the American Law Institute.

She graduated, magna cum laude, from Princeton University, and from New York University School of Law, where she had a Root-Tilden Scholarship for her commitment to public service.

linkedin.com/in/julie-brill-3326512a/

Dawn Cappelli
@DawnCappelli

Fighting cyber threats since 2001 - in spare time LOVE our cabin in the mountain - nothing beats sitting by the campfire next to the stream!!

Dawn Cappelli, CISSP, is VP, Global Security and CISO at Rockwell Automation. Her team, Global and Information Security (G&IS), is responsible for protecting Rockwell Automation and its ecosystem of customers, suppliers, distributors, and partners from the ever-changing global threat landscape.

She is a member of the RSA Conference Advisory Board, the RSA Conference Program Committee, and co-founder of the Open Source Insider Threat information sharing group.

Prior to Rockwell Automation, she was technical manager and then principal engineer for CERT, Software Engineering Institute, Carnegie Mellon University, for more than 25 years.

Dawn was named Pittsburgh CISO of the Year in 2018 and received the Society of Women Engineers Global Team Leadership Award in 2016.

Palo Alto Networks inducted "The CERT Guide to Insider Threats: How to Prevent, Detect, and Respond to Information Technology Crimes," by Dawn Cappelli, Andrew Moore, and Randall Trzeciak, into the Cybersecurity Canon in April 2016.

linkedin.com/in/
dawn-cappelli-cissp-a329505/

Lesley Carhart
@hacks4pancakes

DFIR @dragosinc TOC, martial artist, gamer, marksman, humanist, Lv13 Neutral Good rogue. I write & tweet *very serious* things about infosec. Thoughts are mine.

Lesley Carhart is recognized as a subject matter expert in cybersecurity incident response. She is principal threat leader at Dragos. She spent the last nine years of her 19-year IT career specializing in information security, with a heavy focus on response to nation-state adversaries.

Previously, she served as the incident response team lead at Motorola Solutions, performing security monitoring, digital forensics, and incident-handling services for both enterprise and public safety radio customers.

Lesley regularly speaks at industry conferences and universities, as well as to news media, about security education and career development. She co-organizes resume writing and mock interview clinics at information security conferences to help develop the next generation of security professionals.

In 2017, she was named a Top Woman in Cybersecurity by CyberScoop news, was a keynote speaker at BSides Salt Lake City, and received the Guidance Enfuse Conference Women in Technology award.

Lesley currently serves in the U.S. Air Force Reserves.

linkedin.com/in/lcarhart/

Cindi Carter
@CindiBCarter

Information Security Leader @ MedeAnalytics, Founding President @WomenSecurityKC, @Michigan @UMICHFootball fan, Former leader @BlueKC, @Cerner, @UMich, @Novell

Cindi Carter is a security executive with more than 15 years of experience leading large-scale strategic initiatives. She joined MedeAnalytics as chief security officer in November 2018. As CSO, she oversees global enterprise security, advances a culture of accountability, and protects people, information assets, data, and technologies for MedeAnalytics and its clients.

Cindi is also founder and past president of Women in Security — Kansas City, a non-profit organization with the mission of supporting women in information security at all career levels. She is an advisor to several security organizations and mentor to students and professionals.

She previously served as the deputy CISO at Blue Cross and Blue Shield of Kansas City, where she led vulnerability management, threat intelligence, and cyber resilience. Prior to that, she was senior manager of Enterprise Security at Cerner.

Cindi was named as SC Media Magazine's Women to Watch in Cyber Security 2018.

linkedin.com/in/cindibcarter/

Joy Chik
@joychik

Corporate VP, Microsoft Identity: Azure Active Directory, Office365, Microsoft Account, Xbox, Skype, more | Board member @AnitaB_org | Yoga | Hiking

Joy Chik is corporate vice president of the Identity Division in Microsoft's Cloud + AI group, which helps twenty million organizations and over a billion people secure their digital identities against increasingly pervasive and sophisticated cyber threats. Twenty-five billion times a day, users of Microsoft's cloud services (Azure, Windows, Office 365, Outlook.com, Xbox Live, and Bing) authenticate their identities through the technology that Joy and her organization have created.

Because cybersecurity is a responsibility that has a profound impact on everyday lives, Joy is passionate about cultivating diverse perspectives to find creative solutions to some of the industry's most complex problems.

Joy and her team are pioneering ways to make security more intuitive, such as eliminating passwords, while also championing multiple efforts within the industry to elevate privacy to an equal level of importance as security.

The team she leads is also architecting solutions to help balance control over personal information and the responsibility to protect it between individuals and organizations.

linkedin.com/in/joy-chik-9813305/

Diana-Lynn Contesti
@rougerider

Opinions, etc are mine alone

Diana-Lynn Contesti is a security leader, change agent, author, and internationally known speaker who works to increase aware- ness and understanding of industrial control systems. She provides clear strategies that allow information technology and operat- ing technology departments to co-exist and provide a clear path for them to follow. She has been able to leverage her passion, vision, and energy to develop robust, repeatable information security programs for local and global organizations.

Diana has spoken on various security topics but more recently works to assist organiza- tions in understanding how the Internet of Things will affect them. She is a past chair (2010, 2011) of the (ISC)2 Board of Directors and sponsored Women in Technology Schol- arships. She is an active volunteer and has mentored many people new to the field.

Diana co-chairs the (ISC)2 Advisory Council of North America. She has been recognized as one of the Top Fifty Women in Internet Security and was awarded the James R. Wade Award for her volunteer efforts in advancing information security.

linkedin.com/in/
diana-lynn-contesti-66a8571/

Edna Conway
@Edna_Conway

Chief Security Officer, Global Value Chain at Cisco Systems, Inc. Driving Security through the ICT 3rd Party Ecosystem.

Edna Conway serves as Cisco's chief security officer, global value chain, creating clear strategies to deliver secure operating models for the digital economy. She has built new organizations delivering cybersecurity, compliance, risk management, and value chain transformation. She drives a comprehensive security architecture across Cisco's third-party ecosystem.

She is acknowledged domestically (US Presidential Commissions) and globally (NATO) as the developer of value chain security architectures. She serves on the Executive Committee of the U.S. Department of Homeland Security's ICT Supply Chain Risk Management Task Force.

Acknowledgement of her industry leadership includes membership in the Fortune Most Powerful Women community and several awards including CSO of the Year Award at RSA. She serves on the security advisory board of MassTLC and the board of directors for the International Consortium of Minority Cybersecurity Professionals.

Prior to Cisco, Edna was a partner in an international private legal practice and served as New Hampshire's assistant attorney general. Her speaking venues have included government, academic, and industry forums. Her work has also been featured in a range of publications.

linkedin.com/in/ednaconway/
blogs.cisco.com/author/ednaconway

Anita D'Amico
@AnitaDamico

cybersecurity, application security and Code Dx evangelist, visualization, decision analytics, gardening, Yankees baseball, science fiction

Anita D'Amico is CEO at Code Dx, a trending application security company. She is an experimental psychologist who "wandered into cybersecurity more than 20 years ago through an unusual series of events." She did research for the Merchant Marine, worked on the Space Station project, and then started Northrop Grumman's first information warfare team.

Code Dx's software suite grew from research funded by the Department of Homeland Security, Science and Technology Directorate's Small Business Initiative Research (SBIR) program. Anita founded the Secure Decisions division of Applied Visions, which carried out this research. Code Dx was spun out as a new company to make the results of that research available to the application development community.

Anita is the director of Secure Decisions, which has received more than $20 million in grant funding from various government agencies under her tenure. She in turn takes the products designed in Secure Decisions and commercializes them for Code Dx. She works ardently to position Code Dx's flagship product for application vulnerability management.

linkedin.com/in/anita-d-amico-1a1b515/

Laura Deaner
@B3dwin

Cyber security everywhere! Tweets are my own.

Laura Deaner is the VP and CISO for S&P Global. She leads security governance and enterprise-wide risk management practices. This includes evaluating and monitoring enterprise security risks, establishing common standards for risk mitigation, and providing security oversight and governance. With eighteen years of experience protecting multi-national corporations from threats, Laura was hired as the first female CISO at S&P Global in June 2016.

She transitioned from PR Newswire, where she was responsible for the vision, strategy, and execution of all aspects of information security. In that role, she established the information security program based on the ISO 27001/2 framework and successfully led the company through the aftermath of a major cybersecurity attack.

Laura was previously with Morgan Stanley for six years, as VP and global head of Security Architecture and then VP of IT Security Strategy and Consulting. Prior to that, she was a security analyst for JPMorgan Chase and Citigroup.

linkedin.com/in/ldeaner/

Deneen DeFiore
@deneendefiore

SVP, global chief information & product security officer for GE Aviation

Deneen DeFiore is SVP, global chief information & product security officer for GE Aviation, a company with over 55,000 employees in 80 sites around the globe. She is responsible for securing GE Aviation's business operations, products, information and assets, as well as ensuring compliance to global regulations. Deneen serves as the technical expert and advisor to GE's most senior leaders on cyber risk related to products, services, and ongoing operations.

She began her career with GE in 2001 as IT program manager, Service Delivery. Her roles have included CIO, Energy Services, Industrial Services & Motors, GE Energy; and executive CISO, GE Information Security Technology Center, GE.

Deneen is GE Champion of the Executive Women's Forum and a board member of the Aviation Information Sharing and Analysis Center. She co-leads GE Girls, a summer camp designed to teach young women about STEM-based careers.

Deneen initially studied biology. She got into IT by accident while interning at a healthcare system and taught herself to code.

linkedin.com/in/deneendefiore/

Sherrod DeGrippo
@sherrod_im

I like pics of dogs and #InfoSec memes, tweet those things at me. I also love public enterprise breach response.

Sherrod DeGrippo is director of Threat Research and Detection at Proofpoint, an enterprise security company.

Previously, she was manager of Security Business Services at Nexum, where her job included leading the information security professional services practice for penetration testing, web application assessment, risk assessment, and security consulting.

Sherrod was also senior solutions engineer for Symantec, a senior security consultant for Secureworks, and senior network security analyst for the National Nuclear Security Administration (NNSA).

She completed the Kauffman Foundation's FastTrac program for startup entrepreneurs. She holds several professional certifications and previously held a Top Secret or "Q" clearance.

Sherrod has been a travel/remote employee and consultant for several years and says she has condensed working from home and traveling down to a finely balanced science.

She is also the executive director of Digital Love Atlanta, whose mission is to improve the lives of Atlanta's residents and visitors through the use of cutting edge technology.

linkedin.com/in/sherroddegrippo/

Michelle Dennedy
@mdennedy

VP & Chief Privacy Officer at Cisco. Co-author of The Privacy Engineer's Manifesto. These are my own views & wonderings.

Michelle Finneran Dennedy is VP and chief privacy officer at Cisco, where she works to raise awareness and create tools that promote privacy, quality, respect, trust, and asset-level possibilities for data.

A unique visionary in the field of privacy and the IT industry, she brings together multifaceted approaches for sincere privacy protections that drive business value. She hosts Cisco's Privacy Sigma Riders podcast (cisco.com/go/riders), which focuses on cybersecurity, trust, and data privacy.

She has led security and privacy initiatives at companies including McAfee / Intel Security, Oracle, and Sun Microsystems.

Michelle co-authored "The Privacy Engineer's Manifesto: Getting from Policy to Code to QA to Value."

She has been honored with industry awards including California's Most Powerful and Influential Women, by the National Diversity Council; the IAPP Vanguard Award; and World Women Awards Silver Winner for Female Executive of the Year for her leadership in optimizing Cisco's privacy maturity.

blogs.cisco.com/author/michelledennedy
linkedin.com/in/michelledennedy

Limor Elbaz
@LimorElbaz

Founder & CEO @Peerlyst. Salad master. #InfoSec Lover. Never buy water!

Limor Elbaz is the founder and CEO of Peerlyst, a community of security professionals serving more than half a million security experts in 191 countries. She previously served as VP of corporate development at Imperva (NYSE: IMPV), where she took a leadership role prior to the IPO and in the spin-off of Incapsula.

She led the expansion of Finjan, a web security company, from Israel to the U.S., and led the Malicious Code Research Center, where she also created key patents for the company (acquired by Trustwave).

Limor founded Discretix Technologies (aka Sansa Security) where she brought encryption to mass use by cellular phones, and the company was acquired by ARM for $70 million. Early on, she ran the IT and security of Intel in Israel.

Limor served for six years in an elite technological unit in the Israeli Air Force. She now advises many security companies and serves as a mentor for MACH37 Cyber Accelerator, Girls Who Code, and other initiatives helping younger women get into the security space.

Limor is a lawyer in Israel and New York and an engineer. She holds an MBA from Bar-Ilan University.

linkedin.com/in/limorelbaz/

Elena Elkina
@el0chka

Privacy and Data Protection Geek | Public Speaker | Co-founder/Leadership Board, Women in Security and Privacy | Partner, Aleada Consulting

Elena Elkina is a partner and privacy & data protection management executive at Aleada Consulting. She advises clients on privacy, data protection, and information security issues.

Elena is known for her entrepreneurial approach to driving business performance while protecting information and serving as a trusted adviser for her clients. During her 20-year legal career, she has worked with financial and healthcare institutions, software and Internet companies, major law firms, and the government sector on both international and domestic levels.

Over the past decade, Elena has focused on creating enterprise-level global privacy and data protection programs, including developing and implementing data protection policies, maturity models, and long-term roadmaps; designing and implementing de-identification and data handling strategies and processes; and building privacy and security training and awareness programs.

She is a co-founder and vice chair of Women in Security and Privacy (WISP) and serves on the board of Leading Women in Technology (LWT).

linkedin.com/in/elenaelkina/

Heather Engel
@HeatherEngel5

Chief Strategy Officer at @Sera-Brynn, questioner, woman in tech, mom, yoga teacher, Crossfitter. Tweets are my own.

Heather Engel has nineteen years of experience in cybersecurity, with emphasis on cyber risk management. She has held the role of chief strategy officer at Sera-Brynn since 2013. She provides cybersecurity as part of a greater risk management strategy to clients across a wide variety of industries including non-profit, healthcare, government, retail, and financial. She develops service offerings to solve compliance issues, specifically FedRAMP and the NIST Cybersecurity Framework, DFARS Rule 78, PCI, GDPR, and 23 NYCRR 500.

She also provides business continuity strategy and crisis management in response to data breaches and incidents. Prior to Sera-Brynn, she was lead associate at Booz Allen Hamilton for six years.

Heather served as senior C4ISR analyst for General Dynamics and was an information assurance officer and network security manager for Titan Corporation. She is a current board member of the Virginia Economic Development Partnership (VEDP).

linkedin.com/in/heather-engel-5559335/

Dr. Amelia Estwick
@DrCyberACE

Cybersecurity Thought Leader - Been in the game for over 20 years! Passionate about diversity and inclusion in STEAM #helloworld

Dr. Amelia Estwick is the program director at the National Cybersecurity Institute, an academic, training, and research center dedicated to helping government, industry, military, and academic sectors meet today's challenges in cybersecurity policy, technology, and education. She provides thought leadership for NCI's cybersecurity, academic, research, and training initiatives. She is also the program director for the Master's in Cybersecurity program at Excelsior College where she has taught several different information technology and cybersecurity courses at both undergraduate and graduate levels.

Dr. Estwick has over 20 years of experience in the computer security / cybersecurity field within the intelligence community. She joined the National Security Agency in 1999 as a computer science researcher and held the roles of global network exploitation & vulnerability analyst, senior cybersecurity analyst, operations manager, and division technical director within NSA's Threat Operations Center. She served in the U.S. Army during the Gulf War as a telecommunications center operator.

She currently serves as the vice president for the Women in Cybersecurity Mid-Atlantic Affiliate.

linkedin.com/in/drameliaestwick/

Siobhan Gorman
@Gorman_Siobhan

Advising companies on privacy & cyber issues for @BrunswickGroup. Former Intelligence Correspondent @WSJ. Juggler. Wine enthusiast. Kisser of boo-boos.

Siobhan Gorman is a partner in the Washington, D.C. office of the Brunswick Group, where she concentrates on crisis, cybersecurity, public affairs, and media relations. She has worked on corporate crisis across a range of industries, including financial services, healthcare, defense, entertainment, technology, and automotive. She's led a range of cybersecurity, public affairs, litigation, and corporate reputation projects in the financial, retail, airline, and technology sectors. She regularly advises clients on media relations issues and conducts media training for executives.

Siobhan is a member of the Senior Advisory Group for Harvard University's Defending Digital Democracy Project, focused on preventing and mitigating cyberattacks on the election process. She's also a member of the Advisory Committee for Brown University's Executive Master in Cybersecurity. She previously hosted a weekly consumer cybersecurity segment on local CBS stations called "Eye on Cyber."

Prior to joining Brunswick, she had a successful 17-year career as a reporter, most recently at The Wall Street Journal. She won the 2006 Sigma Delta Chi Award for Washington Correspondence for her coverage of the National Security Agency and was nominated three times for the Pulitzer Prize.

linkedin.com/in/siobhan-gorman-9616a5/

Julie Inman Grant
@tweetinjules

Aussie eSafety Commissioner. Former Tweep, Microsoftie & Adobean. M3 (Massively Multitasking Mum of 3). Proponent of "safety by design." Random musings my own.

Australian eSafety Commissioner Julie Inman Grant promotes online safety for all Australians. The Office of the eSafety Commissioner provides educational resources underpinned by evidence-based research and reporting and take down services for young Australians experiencing serious cyberbullying, for image-based abuse and for illegal content online, including child sexual abuse and abhorrent violent material. Through eSafety Women, they empower women to take control of their online experiences and effectively manage technology risks and abuse.

Julie has extensive experience in the non-profit and government sectors and has held senior public policy and safety roles in the tech industry. As Adobe's director of government relations, APAC, she managed government relations, public policy, and public sector support functions across the Asia Pacific region.

She was vice chairman of the board of the Asia Internet Coalition, and was with Microsoft for 17 years, serving as one of the company's first and longest-standing government relations professionals, ultimately in the role of global safety director. She led Twitter's public policy for Australia and SE Asia and conceptualized and piloted Position of Strength, Twitter's global female safety and empowerment program.

linkedin.com/in/julie-inman-grant-0637035/

Aanchal Gupta
@nchlgpt

Director of Security, Facebook

Aanchal Gupta is the head of security for Facebook's blockchain initiative. Previously, she led a global team responsible for assessing and mitigating security risks across Facebook and its family of apps including WhatsApp, Instagram, Messenger, and Oculus.

Prior to joining Facebook, she was CISO at Microsoft for Skype and Skype for Business. In this role, she managed several broad areas, including security, privacy, compliance, online safety, anti-abuse, and business continuity.

Before joining Microsoft, Aanchal led Yahoo's Global Identity team, contributing to various authentication and authorization open standards such as OpenID and OAuth.

Aanchal was named one of Business Insider's "Most powerful female engineers of 2018." She is a member of the Internet Security Research Group Board of Directors, and a fellow at the RSA (Royal Society for the encouragement of Arts, Manufactures and Commerce).

She serves on technical advisory boards for security startups, CloudKnox Security Inc. and ThreatWatch Inc. She is passionate about building diverse teams and serves on the review board for the Grace Hopper, Enigma, and Black Hat conferences.

linkedin.com/in/aanchalgupta/

Kyla Guru
@*GuruDetective*

Founder/CEO, Bits N' Bytes Cybersecurity, @girlconchicago | @facebook CLP fellow | Stanford @sheplusplus fellow | @NCWITAIC Awardee | #security supergirl

Kyla Guru, a junior at Deerfield High School in Deerfield, Illinois, is the founder of Bits N' Bytes Cybersecurity Education Corp., a national nonprofit with the mission of training and preparing citizens for cyber threats through supplemental curriculum and community engagement.

Kyla started her tech journey "at the age of 7 by learning Scratch, Web Design, and Lego Mindstorms." She discovered her passion for cybersecurity the summer before her freshman year.

Kyla has shared her message for empowering other vulnerable populations on stages including TEDxChicago, NIST's NICE Conference, and the RSA Conference.

In addition to her passion for STEM, shown through her national recognition as a 2019 Facebook Community Leadership Fellow, 2018 NCWIT National Winner, and 2018 Global Teen Leader, Kyla also aims to inspire other teenagers to catalyze social change.

She is the co-founder and co-director of GirlCon Chicago, Chicago's premiere high-school technology conference, uniting over 300 young women in discussing how we can bridge the apparent gender gap in technology and leadership.

linkedin.com/in/kyla-g/

Kim Hakim
@futurecon2019

Your Cyber Security Conference HQ

Kim Hakim is CEO and founder of Future-Con, an exciting new lineup of next generation cybersecurity conferences. With over 20 years in the cybersecurity industry, Kim has the expertise, connections, and vision to deliver a world-class event series designed for cutting-edge cybersecurity education and the latest cybersecurity trends.

Kim is the former founder and CEO of Data Connectors, which organized and hosted tech security conferences in dozens of cities throughout the U.S. and Canada under her leadership. Her accomplishments in creating, managing, and hosting thousands of cybersecurity events for almost two decades throughout North America gained support from industry-leading companies such as McAfee, IBM, Kaspersky, Checkpoint, Watch-Guard, and many more.

Kim is a U.S. Navy veteran and a mother of three. She is also a very active philanthropist in her community. She serves on the board of directors of the Easter Seals Midwest, and she served on the board of directors for the Junior League of St. Louis early on in her career.

linkedin.com/in/kim-hakim-3745b811/

Moriah Hara

@MoriahLazarHara

Global CISO, Board Member, Investor. Moriah Hara brings over nineteen years of information security and management experience.

Moriah Hara currently is a CISO advisory member for ClearSky Security Fund and Glilot Capital Partners. Previously, she was the CISO of IPG & Wells Fargo Capital Markets. At Wells Fargo, she had security accountability for all aspects of the investment banking division that generated approximately $4 billion per year. She built the global VISA Payment Card Industry QSA (Qualified Security Assessor) program, engineered the global vulnerability management program at Credit Suisse Networks and co-created the Threat Management team at Bank of America. She has also spoken in front of Fortune 50 audiences on topics such as Data Leakage Prevention, Payment Security and Risks to Unstructured Data. She was the ISE Northeast CISO Executive of the Year Finalist in 2017.

Moriah is a graduate of Harvard University's Executive Cyber Security Program and has over 19 years of IS industry experience. She also holds an extensive set of security and technical certifications including CSSLP, CISSP, CISM, PCI QSA and MCSE. Most recently, she has been leading cybersecurity badges for Girl Scouts of various ages as well as sponsoring and mentoring urban young adults towards cybersecurity careers through the Year Up program.

linkedin.com/in/moriah-hara-a18b84/

Meredith R. Harper
@mrhciso

A Security Evangelist passionate about protecting what's most important, our PEOPLE and our PATIENTS!

Meredith R. (Phillips) Harper joined Eli Lilly & Company in August 2018 as their deputy CISO and transitioned to the role of CISO for Lilly's global information security program in April 2019.

Meredith was the chief information privacy and security officer for Henry Ford Health System for almost 16 years. She had leadership responsibility for Information & Network Security Services, Information Privacy Services, Privacy & Security Risk Management Services, as well as Identity & Access Management Services. She had ultimate responsibility for the protection of Henry Ford's provider, insurance, retail, and research businesses.

Meredith is an active member of the Health Care Compliance Association and the International Association of Privacy Professionals (IAPP). She holds dual certifications in healthcare compliance and privacy and is certified as a healthcare information security and privacy practitioner and a certified information security manager.

She is passionate about empowering women and minorities to embark upon careers in technology, especially in information security where those populations are not very well represented.

linkedin.com/in/deputyciso/

Del Harvey
@delbius

VP, Twitter Trust & Safety; personal account. These views are mine (but could also be yours).

As VP of Trust & Safety at Twitter, Del Harvey leads an international team to define and enforce policy and ensure safety and security for everyone on Twitter in the challenging realm of modern social media.

She states that her job is to ensure user trust, protect user rights, and keep users safe — both from each other and, at times, from themselves. Del and her team work closely with virtually every department at Twitter — including BD, Comms, Engineering, Legal, Media, Product, and Public Policy — and participate in a number of industry initiatives within the spaces of legal policy and online safety.

Del has been with Twitter for ten years. Previously, she spent five years as the law enforcement liaison for a group fighting child sexual exploitation, where she worked with agencies ranging from local police departments to the FBI, U.S. Marshals, and the Secret Service.

Del is also a member of the advisory board for INHOPE, the international association of Internet hotlines. She frequently speaks at events, including Google's Big Tent, SXSW, FOSI, Microsoft's Social Research Symposium, SMX, and TED.

linkedin.com/in/delharvey/

Melissa Hathaway
@CyberReadyIndex

Cyber Readiness Index 2.0 documents the core components of cyber readiness in a blueprint for nations to follow. Hathaway Global Strategies LLC & @PotomacInst

Melissa Hathaway is a leading expert in cyberspace policy and cybersecurity. She served in two U.S. presidential administrations, spearheading the Cyberspace Policy Review for President Barack Obama and leading the Comprehensive National Cybersecurity Initiative (CNCI) for President George W. Bush.

As president of Hathaway Global Strategies LLC, she brings a multi-disciplinary and multi-institutional perspective to strategic consulting and strategy formulation for public and private sector clients.

Having served on the board of directors for three public companies and three non-profit organizations, and as a strategic advisor to a number of public and private companies, Melissa brings a unique combination of policy and technical expertise, as well as boardroom experience to help others better understand the intersection of government policy, developing technological and industry trends, and economic drivers that impact acquisition and business development strategy in this field.

Melissa publishes regularly on cybersecurity matters affecting companies and countries.

belfercenter.ksg.harvard.edu/experts/2132/melissa_hathaway.html

Tammy Hawkins
@HawkinsTammy

Loves IT security and dogs with big ears. STL, MO gal living in Dublin, Ireland. VP Cyber & Intelligence @MasterCard, views my own. Connect w/me on LinkedIn.

Tammy Hawkins is VP, Software Engineering, Cyber & Intelligence at Mastercard. Tammy has been with Mastercard for more than 10 years. As VP, Software Development, Commercial Solutions, a role she held for two years, she spearheaded the design and development of a world-class B2B commercial virtual card payments system marshalling resources of a global team spread across multiple geographies from the current location at Dublin, Ireland.

Other tasks included formulating rules and mechanisms for fraud deterrence, which encompasses In Control for Commercial Payments, In Control for Business Travel, Mastercard Payment Gateway, and Straight Through Payments.

Tammy also led a diverse and large 100+ multinational team composed of a vast array of skills such as directors, architects, and software development contractors and employees located in Ireland, the U.S., Malaysia, and Brazil.

Prior to that position, she was VP, Authentication Software Engineering, Enterprise Security Solutions.

linkedin.com/in/tammyhawkinslinked/

Mary Haynes
@maryhayneskc

VP Network Security, Charter Communications

Mary Haynes is a founding board member of Women in Security — Denver, dedicated to advancing the leadership, solidarity, and professional development of women in the field of cybersecurity.

She is also the VP of Network Security at Charter Communications. She currently leads the network security program for Charter's core networks and services, including high speed Internet, telephony, and video products. Her team is responsible for security standards, compliance, vulnerability and risk assessments, event monitoring, and incident response. Her team is also responsible for Charter's Law Enforcement Response Team, abuse management, and botnet remediation programs.

Mary was previously director of security services for Westar Energy. As CSO, she was responsible for leading cyber and physical security teams.

Prior to that, she was senior manager at CenturyLink, where she led a team of 12 information security engineers and managers. She has also held the positions of network security specialist at Sprint Nextel, manager of IT Security at Birch Telecom, and regional security manager at AT&T.

linkedin.com/in/marykhaynes/

Emily Heath
@CISOEmilyHeath

Chief Information Security Officer at United Airlines. Lover of food, travel, technology, art and everything creative! Opinions are my own.

Emily Heath is the CISO and VP of United Airlines. She is responsible for information security, risk and compliance programs globally. Her responsibilities include all strategic direction and execution of security programs and initiatives across the company and its 90,000 employees. Her teams won CSO50 awards in 2016, 2017, and 2019.

She was one of Crain's Tech 50 in 2018 and was included in HMG Strategy's 2019 Top 100 Technology Executives to Watch Awards.

Emily is a speaker at leading industry conferences and events. She is a member of the board of advisors for venture capital fund Cyberstarts and a board member of the Aviation Information Sharing and Analysis Center (A-ISAC), the National Technology Security Council (NTSC), and the Security Advisor Alliance.

She is a former police detective from the UK Financial Crimes Unit where she led investigations into international investment fraud, money laundering, and large scale identity theft cases. She ran joint investigations with the FBI, SEC, and London's Serious Fraud Office.

linkedin.com/in/eheath1/

Rebecca Herold
@PrivacyProf

Infosec, privacy, IT | Tech Entrepreneur | President, SIMBUS360 | CEO, Rebecca Herold & Assoc, LLC aka The Privacy Professor | Expert witness | THIS IS MY ONLY TWITTER ID

Rebecca Herold, FIP, CISSP, CIPM, CIPP/US, CIPT, CISM, CISA, FLMI, has more than 25 years of IT, infosec, and privacy experience. She is the founder of SIMBUS, LLC, an all-in-one SaaS business solution for privacy, security, compliance and cyber insurance.

Since 2004, she has also owned Rebecca Herold, LLC aka The Privacy Professor, which provides information security, privacy, IT, and compliance consulting services and products.

Rebecca is the host of Data Security and Privacy with the Privacy Professor, a radio program / podcast on VoiceAmerica.

She serves as an expert witness for information security, privacy, and compliance topics. She also enjoys delivering keynote speeches (on five continents so far … she's shooting for all seven!).

Rebecca has authored 19 books to date. She was an adjunct professor for the Norwich University MS in Information Security & Assurance Program for nine years.

linkedin.com/in/rebeccaherold/
privacyguidance.com
voiceamerica.com/show/2733/data-security-and-privacy-with-the-privacy-professor

Kelly Jackson Higgins
@kjhiggins

Executive Editor at Dark Reading, but most of my family and friends have no clue what I do. My opinions posted here are mine only.

Kelly Jackson Higgins is the executive editor of Dark Reading, a leading cybersecurity news site and community. She is responsible for the day-to-day news operation, including assigning and editing stories and reporting and writing content. She is also responsible for supporting content and planning and moderating sessions for Dark Reading's parent company UBM's online and live events, including Interop and Black Hat.

Kelly began her career as a sports writer. She has been a journalist in the IT field for more than two and a half decades. She has reported and edited for publications including Network Computing, Secure Enterprise Magazine, Communications Week, Virginia Business magazine, and other major media properties. She began her career with Dark Reading in 2006.

Kelly has served as a speaker for various regional cybersecurity events. She was named as one of Folio's 2019 Top Women in Media and named as SANS Top 10 Cybersecurity Journalists in 2012, 2014, and 2018.

She holds a bachelor's degree from William & Mary.

linkedin.com/in/kellyj2/

Marcia Hofmann
@marciahofmann

Digital rights defender. Founder of Zeitgeist Law (https://zeitgeist.law). Special counsel to @EFF. Teach at @ColoLaw.

Marcia Hofmann is a digital rights lawyer and founder and principal of Zeitgeist Law PC. Her law practice focuses on computer crime, information security, electronic privacy, free expression, open government, and intellectual property.

She has had a relationship with the Electronic Frontier Foundation for 13 years. Marcia has been special counsel since 2013 and is a collaborator on certain EFF projects. She served as senior staff attorney between 2010 and 2013. She litigated cases involving a wide range of technology issues, including electronic privacy, computer crime and security, free speech, and intermediary immunity matters. She also counseled technology companies and researchers on compliance with communications surveillance and intellectual property statutes.

Marcia is also a member of the board of directors of Without My Consent, a non-profit organization seeking to combat online invasions of privacy.

She is an adjunct professor at the University of Colorado School of Law.

linkedin.com/in/marciahofmann

Sarah (Merrion) Isaacs
@312isaacs

Founder and COO of Conventus Corporation

Sarah Isaacs is founder and COO of Conventus Corporation, a cybersecurity software company that offers infosec consulting and focuses on providing the visibility needed to track and reduce risk. They accomplish that through NorthStar, a holistic system that provides asset detection and inventory capabilities, configuration, vulnerability stats reporting, and intelligence for measuring risk management effectiveness.

Sarah is also an advisory board member of the International Consortium of Minority Cybersecurity Professionals (ICMCP), whose goal is to achieve the consistent representation of women and minorities in cybersecurity through programs designed to foster recruitment, inclusion and retention.

Previously, she was consulting services technical manager at Symantec and a security engineer at Arthur Anderson.

Sarah is passionate about promoting women in technology and writes often on the subject. She was most recently featured in Fast Company, VentureBeat, Women 2.0, SC Magazine, and Huffington Post.

linkedin.com/in/sarahmerrionisaacs/

Lisa Jiggetts
@lisajiggetts

Fulltime geek, lifetime artist. Marine Wifey. AF Veteran. Blasian made in Japan. Cyberjutsu. Love to eat.

Lisa Jiggetts is the founder and president of the Women's Society of Cyberjutsu (WSC), which provides women with the resources and support required to enter and advance as a cybersecurity professional.

WSC uses a holistic approach to develop programs that train women in the hard technical skills and soft skills, leaving them feeling empowered to succeed. Lisa is known as a straight-up but down-to-earth motivator with the women whom she mentors. She and her organization have been profiled in Fortune Magazine, SC Magazine, and PenTest Magazine, among others.

She has been a guest speaker for numerous conferences and recorded podcasts. A service-disabled veteran, she began her cyber career in the military where she was an IT security specialist.

With over 20 years of information technology experience, 17 of which are in cybersecurity, her experience spans risk assessments, penetration testing, vulnerability assessments, and policy development across military, government, and commercial industries. Lisa is also an accomplished artist.

linkedin.com/in/wsccyberjin/

Neira Jones
@neirajones

Advisor | Speaker | Payments | Innovation | Fintech | Security | I make it happen... https://www.instagram.com/neiraj0nes/ https://www.youtube.com/neirajones

Neira Jones is an independent advisor and international speaker who advises organizations on payments, fintech, regtech, cybercrime, information security, regulations, and digital innovation.

She is a non-executive director for Nasdaq-listed cybersecurity firm Cognosec. She also chairs the advisory board for mobile innovator Ensygnia. She is a partner for the Global Cyber Alliance and an ambassador for the Emerging Payments Association.

Neira's recent recognitions include Thomson Reuters UK's Top 30 Social influencers in Risk, Compliance and Regtech 2017; The Planet Compliance Top 50 RegTech Influencers; the Jax Finance Top 20 Social Influencers in Fintech 2017; the Richtopia Top 100 Most Influential People in Fintech; Tripwire's Top Influencer in Security to Follow on Twitter 2015; and CEOWorld magazine's Top Chief Security Officer to Follow on Twitter 2014.

She is an Infosecurity Europe Hall of Fame alumni. She has served on the PCI SSC Board of Advisors for four years and is a fellow of the British Computer Society.

Neira previously worked for Barclaycard, Santander, Abbey National, Oracle Corp., and Unisys.

linkedin.com/in/neirajones/

Diana Kelley
@dianakelley14

Cybersecurity CTO, security architect, keynote speaker, author, strategist. I work at Microsoft. My tweets are mine.

Diana Kelley is the cybersecurity field CTO for Microsoft and a cybersecurity architect, executive advisor, and author. At Microsoft, she leverages her 25+ years of cyber-risk and security experience to provide advice and guidance to CSOs, CIOs, and CISOs at some of the world's largest companies. She is also a contributor to the Microsoft Security Intelligence Report (SIR).

In addition to her work at Microsoft, she serves on the ACM Ethics & Plagiarism Committee and is an industry mentor at Cybersecurity Factory, a summer program for security startups.

Diana is a guest lecturer at Boston College's Master of Science in Cybersecurity program. She is also CTO and director of the non-profit Sightline Security.

She is a member of the RSA US Program Committee for 2018 and 2019 and was an IEEE "Rock Star of Risk" in 2016. She keynotes frequently at major conferences and co-authored the book, "Cryptographic Libraries for Developers."

Diana previously worked at IBM where she built and managed the IBM Security Research publication process.

linkedin.com/in/dianakelleysecuritycurve/

Jill Knesek
@JillKnesek

I'm a passionate security professional with an interest in Cyber Security & Risk Management. And of course views expressed here are my own.

Jill Knesek has more than 20 years of experience in cybersecurity. As CSO for Cheetah Digital, she is responsible for providing enterprise-wide leadership in developing, planning, coordinating, administering, managing, staffing, and supervising all aspects of information security. The scope of responsibilities encompasses development and execution of the security office mission and mandate, office governance, policy development and management, training and awareness, and security project portfolio development.

Jill served as a special agent for the FBI, assigned to the Cyber Crime Squad in the Los Angeles field office. She was the case agent for several high-profile cases, including the infamous Kevin Mitnick and Mafiaboy investigations.

Prior to joining Cheetah Digital, she was the CISO and VP of Information Security for Mattel. She previously held two roles with BT Global Services. She was chief security officer before becoming head of global security practice, BT Advice.

Jill is a frequent industry speaker. She has also written and published several articles and has been recognized often for her service to the security industry.

linkedin.com/in/jillknesek/

Chris Kubecka
@secevangelism

Established security after the world's most devastating cyber warfare attack against Saudi Aramco, author, cyberwar expert, former Space Command USAF

Chris Kubecka is a "cyber crime fighter and cyber war strategist" who has led her share of unusual digital crime incident investigations. She is the founder and CEO of HypaSec, which offers expert advice, incident response management, lecturing, training in IT and ICS security, penetration testing and writing services in security.

Chris is an advisor and subject matter expert to governments and industries. She was brought in to set up a security operation in 2012, when Saudi Aramco (the state-owned national oil company of Saudi Arabia) was hit with the Shamoon logic bomb, a destructive virus that affected 35,000 computers and forced Aramco to take its network offline.

She previously served as IT security manager for Achmea and a client security analyst for Unisys. She has chaired and presented at leading industry conferences and has authored several books regarding computer science and penetration testing, including "Down the Rabbit Hole: An OSINT Journey (Open Source Intelligence Gathering)" and "Hack the World with OSINT (Hackers Gonna Hack)."

Chris served in the U.S. Air Force and with the Space Command before embarking on her cybersecurity career.

linkedin.com/in/chris-k-6577984/

Mischel Kwon
@mkacyber

MKACyber is a venture backed MSSP & security consulting co, with elite SOC expertise, providing a business-first, balanced approach to operational security.

Mischel Kwon is the founder and CEO of MKACyber. She founded the company in 2010 to improve security operations for enterprises and U.S. federal government agencies.

She has more than 35 years of broad IT and security experience, ranging from application design and development, to network architecture and deployment, to building and implementing security operations centers. She built the first Justice Security Operations Center (JSOC) to monitor and defend the Department of Justice network against cyber threats while serving as the deputy director for IT Security Staff at the U.S. Department of Justice.

She started out as a programmer, writing code for IBM mainframes and versions of automated cash registers. She served as VP of Public Sector Security for RSA Security and as director for the U.S. Computer Emergency Readiness Team (US-CERT).

Mischel currently sits on the board of the Western Governors University IT Council. She previously served as an adjunct professor at George Washington University, where she ran the GW Cyber Defense Lab.

linkedin.com/in/mischelkwon/

Lise Lapointe
@LiseLapointe

CEO @ Terranova and Author of The Human Fix to Human Risk TM

Lise Lapointe is the CEO of Terranova Security and author of "The Human Fix to Human Risk." She founded her first IT company with the arrival of PCs, in 1982.

Seven years later, Lise started Microcode, a training center that was acquired by Telus Business Solutions in 1998. She was VP of Training until January 2001.

Her third company, Terranova, was one of the first companies in the world to focus on cybersecurity awareness for businesses. Terranova is recognized as a World Leader in Security Awareness since 2015 (Gartner Magic Quadrant for Security Awareness Computer-based training). Terranova has trained more than 7 million users, in more than 40 languages, for some of the largest employers in the world.

With a vision to be the undisputed security partner of choice for organizations and security leaders globally, Lise surrounds herself with strategic thinkers and has ongoing plans to scale up her company to continue to support organizations and security leaders in their security awareness journey.

She is inspired by women who persevere and make a positive impact in business and in people's lives.

linkedin.com/in/lise-lapointe-bb7b9a1/

Dr. Meg Layton
@Vamegabyte

Mom/Adventurer/traveler/teacher in life and cyberspace. Cybersecurity professional. BtVS occasionally referenced. My own thoughts represented here.

Dr. Margaret (Meg) Layton has been working in the IT industry for over two decades. In 2001, she joined a startup company, Mountain Wave, which was acquired by Symantec. Since then, she has worked in various roles within the company, both on products and on the intelligence that fuels the frontline responders.

She is presently director of engineering for Symantec's Cyber Security Services unit. She works with a team of talented software engineers and security professionals delivering the tools used by the defenders in cyberspace.

Dr. Layton volunteers as a technical mentor for local CyberPatriot organizations. She is also an adjunct professor for colleges and teaching courses in the security field.

Previously, she worked as a director of IT for a telecommunications company doing business in Africa. She maintains several certifications in the cybersecurity realm that she is passionate about, including both the CISSP and CSSLP certifications from ISC(2), and GIAC certifications for incident handling, forensic analysis, and penetration testing.

linkedin.com/in/meglayton/detail/contact-info/

Shannon Lietz
@devsecops

Fusion of DevSec, DevOps and SecOps to make way for secure Innovation

Shannon Lietz has over two decades of experience pursuing advanced security defenses and next generation security solutions, as well as leading and motivating high performing teams. She is currently the DevSecOps leader for Intuit. She is responsible for setting and driving the company's DevSecOps and cloud security strategy, roadmap, and implementation in support of corporate innovation. She operates a 24x7 DevSecOps team that specializes in adversary management.

She received the Scott Cook Innovation Award in 2014 for developing and cultivating an innovation cloud security program to protect sensitive data in AWS. She has significant experience leading crisis management for large-scale security breaches and restoration of services for several Fortune 500 companies.

Prior to joining Intuit, Shannon was senior manager of security at ServiceNow, responsible for the cloud security engineering efforts. She held two positions with Sony and drove the implementation of a new secure data center. She also held security roles with RSM McGladrey and Savvis Communications.

linkedin.com/in/shannonlietz/

Kelly Lum
@aloria

Product and Application Security for @Spotify by day, @NYU_CSE AppSec professor by night. she/her/hers. Clinically depressed and still well dressed.

Kelly Lum is a security engineer at Spotify who says she reads a lot of code and is "excellent at herding cats." She has over a decade of experience in application and network security, from the financial and government sectors to the startup space.

Kelly has been an adjunct professor of Graduate Computer Networking and Application Security at NYU Polytechnic School of Engineering since 2014. She regularly speaks about reverse engineering at various conferences, including Black Hat, SummerCon, and COUNTERMEASURE.

Kelly began her security career in 2003 as a computer science intern at the Air Force Research Laboratory. She was a security engineer in the U.S. Army for two years.

She was an information security analyst with the Federal Reserve Bank of New York for four years before becoming global application security lead of NASDAQ OMX. Her team was responsible for supporting NASDAQ's development organizations throughout the software development life cycle.

She also served as Citi's technical information security officer and senior security engineer at Tumblr. Prior to her position with Spotify, she was security staff architect at Flatiron Health.

linkedin.com/in/tacotuesday/

Mary Mack
@mackmary

CEDS, CISSP, CIAM, CTE, Esq. Coder, way early adopter, privacy, cyber, security, law, tech, Columbia River Gorge, wears black. Exec Dir Assn Certified eDiscovery Specialists.

E-discovery pioneer Mary Mack is the executive director of the Association of Certified E-Discovery Specialists. She has two decades of strong credibility and sound leadership within the e-discovery community and is known for her relationship and community building skills and for the depth of her technical and e-discovery knowledge.

Her clients have included DOJ, FTC, Fortune 100, and most of the AmLaw 100. She previously served as enterprise technology counsel for ZyLAB and corporate technology counsel for Fios.

She is frequently sought out to share her expertise via global conferences and by media for comment on industry issues. Mary has spoken at venues including Gartner Symposium, the American Bar Association International Law Committee, Relativity Fest, Tokyo Summit, Legaltech NYC, and many others.

She is the author of what is considered the first book on e-discovery, "A Process of Illumination: The Practical Guide to Electronic Discovery." She is the co-editor of "eDiscovery for Corporate Counsel" (Thomas Reuters).

linkedin.com/in/marymack/

Heather Mahalik
@HeatherMahalik

Digital Forensics Professional, SANS Senior Instructor and author #FOR585, wife, mama, author, serial vacationer, horse lover and simply over-scheduled!

To say that digital forensics is central to Heather Mahalik's life is an understatement. She has worked on high-stress and high-profile cases, investigating everything from child exploitation to Osama Bin Laden's media. She has almost 17 years of experience in digital forensics, including 10 focused on mobile forensics.

There's hardly a device or platform Heather hasn't researched or examined or a commercial tool she hasn't used. She is the director of Forensic Engineering at ManTech International Corporation. She co-authors and leads SANS' Smartphone Forensic Analysis In-Depth course and blogs at smarterforensics.com.

Heather says she spends most of her time "cracking into tough stuff." Her experience flows into the classroom and her talks. Her students/conference attendees frequently reach out to thank her for her efforts, saying she helped solve cases they've been working.

She says nothing compares to knowing that the effort you put into researching, developing, and sharing something new in the DFIR field "makes the world a better and safer place."

linkedin.com/in/heather-mahalik-gasf-gcfe-cfce-ence-mfce-3615535/

Eve Maler
@xmlgrrl

**XMLgrrl; User-Managed Access @UMAWG
UMAnitarian; @ForgeRock privacy /
consent veep; @ZZAuth_LTs rocker; main
squeeze of @eliasisrael**

Eve Maler is a renowned strategist, innovator, and communicator on digital identity, security, privacy, and consent, with a focus on fostering successful ecosystems and individual empowerment.

As VP of Innovation & Emerging Technology in ForgeRock's Office of the CTO, she drives privacy and consent innovation for the ForgeRock Identity Platform, enabling user-controlled and compliant data sharing across web, mobile, and IoT contexts.

Eve founded and leads the User-Managed Access standards effort and guides implementation of UMA and other privacy and consent solutions. She also directs the company's engagement in interoperability standards such as Health Relationship Trust (HEART) and provides expert advice to public and private forums such as the Facebook/Ctrl-Shift research on A New Paradigm for Personal Data and the U.S. Health and Human Services API Task Force.

Previously, Eve was a principal analyst at Forrester Research, an identity solutions architect with PayPal, and a technology director at Sun Microsystems, where she co-founded and made major contributions to the SAML standard.

In a previous life, she co-invented XML.

linkedin.com/in/evemaler/

Mihoko Matsubara
@M_Miho_JPN

Adjunct Fellow @PacificForum & Associate Fellow @HJS_Org. Cybersecurity policy writer /speaker. Weekly @mainichibiz.

Mihoko Matsubara is chief cybersecurity strategist at NTT Corporation. She previously served as CSO Japan and VP and public sector chief security officer, Asia-Pacific, for Palo Alto Networks. She served the Japanese Ministry of Defense between 2000-2009.

As a member of the Special Committee on Technology-associated Strategy, Japanese Government, she advised the government regarding its cybersecurity strategy. She was Intel's cybersecurity policy director and a senior cybersecurity analyst for Hitachi Systems.

A previous SPF fellow for Pacific Forum CSIS, she has written extensively on Asia-Pacific policy issues and cybersecurity in English and Japanese through Council on Foreign Relations' Asia Unbound, Forbes, Harvard Asia Quarterly, and RUSI Journal.

Mihoko has a weekly column on cybersecurity for the Mainichi Shimbun. A sought-after speaker, she is frequently invited to international conferences to be on a panel or give a presentation regarding cybersecurity policy issues in Asia and international cooperation on cybersecurity or cyber threats, including the NATO CCDCOE CyCon as the first Japanese speaker.

linkedin.com/in/
mihoko-matsubara-8b124124/

Jenna McAuley
@JennaMcAuley

CISO, cybersecurity zealot, headstrong feminist, soccer (football) lover, mother, rabble-rouser and corporate interloper. My views are my own.

Jenna McAuley is vice president of Information Security and Information Technology Oversight at American Express.

Jenna previously served as chief information security officer at Mercer, a global consulting firm. She was responsible for establishing, executing, and maintaining the enterprise vision, strategy, and program to ensure that Mercer's physical and digital information assets and technologies were adequately protected. She employed a number of security awareness training programs, including a blog campaign tied to Cybersecurity Awareness Month.

Her previous roles include cyber threat management at EY. She was with Accenture for 13 years, first as an enterprise business specialist and later as security manager. Her expertise is in the design and delivery of cost-effective, high-performance enterprise security.

Jenna is skilled in all phases of the security life cycle, from application development and code analysis through compliance monitoring, incident management, and remediation. She believes that security is a corporate culture that needs to be in the fabric of everyone's interactions with clients, customers, and data.

linkedin.com/in/jenna-mcauley-18a2855/

Allison Miller
@selenakyle

protects platforms & people online. graphs the grey cybers: econ, risk, fraud, infosec, datasci researcher, designer, artist & mathlete. what the fox says

Allison Miller is SVP Engineering at Bank of America. She leads the engineering efforts for the company's information security organization.

With over 15 years of experience building teams and technology that protect people and platforms, Allison is known for her expertise in designing and implementing real-time risk prevention and detection systems running at Internet-scale.

Prior to her current role, she held technical and leadership roles in security, risk analytics, and payments/commerce at Google, Electronic Arts, Tagged / MeetMe, PayPal / eBay, and Visa International. She was the first person to be officially hired into GlaxoSmithKline's IT Security team, as lead analyst.

Allison speaks internationally on security, fraud and risk. She previously co-chaired the O'Reilly Security Conference and has held board roles with (ISC)2, SIRA, and Keypoint Credit Union.

She is a board trustee for the Center for Cyber Safety and Education, a non-profit charitable trust that works to ensure that people across the globe have a positive and safe experience online through educational programs, scholarships, and research.

linkedin.com/in/allisonmiller/

Jennifer (JJ) Minella
@jjx

Author, Speaker | VP of Engineering & Security | Top 10 Women in Security in SC Magazine | Dancer | Security diva | (ISC)2 Chair | Mindfulness devotee

Jennifer Minella is VP of Engineering and Security and consulting CISO with Carolina Advanced Digital, Inc.

With more than 15 years of experience in the technology industry, her background covers specialized areas of infrastructure security, access control, wireless technologies, and industrial security. In her engineering role, she leads strategic research and consulting for government agencies, educational institutions, and Fortune 100 and 500 corporations.

Jennifer is a published author, editorial contributor, and trusted adviser for information security topics to the media. Her latest work includes the integration of mindfulness techniques and the application of proven leadership techniques for the benefit of infosecurity professionals and industry.

She serves on the international board of directors for (ISC)2 and on steering committees with NCTA's Cyber Security Network and Knowledge Workforce Network. She is also a volunteer mentor with the US AFA CyberPatriot program.

Jennifer is a competitive powerlifter and dancer, including ballroom and swing.

linkedin.com/in/jenniferminella/

Kathleen Moriarty
@KathleeMoriarty

I like open water swimming and #InfoSec memes, tweet those things at me. I also love public enterprise breach response.

Kathleen Moriarty is global lead security architect with Dell EMC Office of the CTO, working on technology strategy and standards. During her tenure in the Office of the CTO, Kathleen served as the IETF security area director from March 2014-2018.

Kathleen is a curriculum advisor at Georgetown University for its SCS MPS Applied Intelligence Program. She is chair of Coordinating Attack Response at Internet Scale (CARIS) workshops aimed at tackling the information security professional deficit.

Prior to assuming her role for Dell EMC, Kathleen achieved over a decade of experience driving positive outcomes across information technology leadership, project management, large teams, process improvement, IT strategy and vision, information security, and operations management in multiple roles with MIT Lincoln Laboratory, FactSet Research Systems, and PSINet.

She holds a Master of Science in computer science from Rensselaer Polytechnic Institute and a Bachelor of Science in mathematics from Siena College.

linkedin.com/in/
kathleen-moriarty-022a062/

Monique Morrow
@moniquejmorrow

Chief Technology Strategist | Groundbreaking Technologist | Proven Innovator

Monique Morrow is a former CTO at Cisco who works tirelessly to align technologies to society's needs. She is president of the VETRI Foundation, whose mission is to empower people to control their identity and privacy.

She is also president and co-founder of the Humanized Internet, which is working to use new technologies to defend the rights of vulnerable people and give every human being worldwide secure, sovereign control over their digital identity. The Humanized Internet is also part of a cross-industry group selected as MIT 2018 Frontline in Health Solvers for Refugee Workforce and Blockchain. The organization was named Tech Non-Profit Organization of the Year (Global) in BWM's 2018 Brand of the Year Awards.

Monique was recognized by One World Identity as one of the Top 100 Influencers in Identify for 2019, Forbes Top 50 Women Globally in Tech 2018, one of the top 50 EMEA Influencers in Data Center and Cloud in June 2017, and one of the top 100 Digital Shapers 2018 in Switzerland.

She is a venture partner of Sparklabs Accelerator for Cybersecurity and Blockchain and is a TEDx speaker and an advisor.

linkedin.com/in/moniquejeannemorrow/

Tammy Moskites
@QueenofCandor

CISO/CIO/Sr Security Exec-God & Family come 1st; Integrity is my foundation; Mentor, Road Warrior, Foodie, Candor is one of my best qualities-These are My Views

Tammy Moskites is a managing director and senior security executive at Accenture. She previously served as CISO of Home Depot and Time Warner Cable. She was global CIO and CISO of Venafi and led their executive advisory board.

She has traveled the globe working with hundreds of CISOs/CIOs and government entities on strategy and foundational security. She is a member of the ISACA Cybersecurity Taskforce and involved in ISACA's She Leads Tech program. She is also a member of the Information Systems Security Association (ISSA), a distinguished fellow with the Ponemon Institute, and an editorial advisor at CISO Magazine.

Tammy is on the list of IFSEC Global Cybersecurity Influencers for 2018. She has been featured in publications including Forbes (Meet the Woman Powering the Fight Against Cybercrime), ZDNet, and CSO magazine.

She is a sought after global speaker in the areas of security and governance, as well as career building and mentoring.

linkedin.com/in/tmoskites/

Emily Mossburg
@EmilyJMossburg

Leader of Deloitte Cyber Advisory and Implementation Services, Principal, Deloitte & Touche LLP. Often quoted, never duplicated. My opinions are my own.

Emily Mossburg is a principal on Deloitte & Touche's Cyber Risk Services Leadership Team. She leads Cyber Risk's Advise & Implement offerings and services including strategy, defense and response; data risk; infrastructure; application security; and identity.

In this capacity, she is responsible for Deloitte's development and delivery of cross-industry services assisting clients to improve their cyber strategy, programs, proactive security posture, and preparedness to identify, respond to and recover from cyber incidents.

Over the last twenty years, Emily has served clients in both the federal and private sectors in developing strategy and programs and implementing technical solutions to manage cyber risk, information security, data protection, and privacy.

With a focus in financial services, she also has experience leading projects with a specific focus on Payment Card Industry Data Security Standard compliance, third party cybersecurity management, and network security and data security risk management.

linkedin.com/in/emilymossburg/

Katie Moussouris
@k8em0

Founder/CEO @LutaSecurity. Bug bounty & vuln dclosure. Hacker. MIT Sloan & Harvard Belfer visiting scholar. @NewAmCyber & @MasonNatSec Fellow. She/her.

Katie Moussouris is the founder and CEO of Luta Security, a company offering unparalleled expertise to create robust vulnerability coordination programs. Luta Security specializes in governments and multi-party supply chain vulnerability coordination.

She recently testified as an expert on bug bounties and the labor market for security research for the U.S. Senate and has also been called upon for European Parliament hearings on dual-use technology.

Katie was later invited by the U.S. State Department to help renegotiate the Wassenaar Arrangement. She successfully helped change the export control language to include technical exemptions for vulnerability disclosure and incident response.

She is a co-author of an economic research paper on the labor market for bugs, published as a book chapter by MIT Press in 2017, and presented on the first system dynamics model of the vulnerability economy and exploit market in 2015, as part of her academic work as a visiting scholar at MIT Sloan School.

Katie previously held security roles with Symantec, HackerOne, and Microsoft, where her work encompassed industry-leading initiatives such as Microsoft's bug bounty programs & Microsoft Vulnerability Research.

linkedin.com/in/kmoussouris/

Isabel Muench
@IsabelMuench

BSI (Bundesamt für Sicherheit in der Informationstechnik), Fachbereichsleiterin Kritische Infrastrukturen

Isabel Muench is an information security expert and works for the German Federal Office for Information Security (BSI - Bundesamt für Sicherheit in der Informationstechnik), whose mission is to promote IT security in Germany. It is the central IT security service provider for the German government but also offers services to IT manufacturers, as well as private and commercial users.

She is head of Branch Critical Instrastructures within the BSI. She has a wide range of experience in advising, evaluating, and auditing information security related issues both in the private and in the public sector. She participates in the national and international discussions in this field and is a well-known author in the area.

Isabel's key activities cover the development and advancement of the IT-Grundschutz and the BSI-Standards on information security management including risk and business continuity management and the coordination of the activities concerning Critical Infrastructure Protection.

She is a fellow of the German Informatics Society (GI).

linkedin.com/in/isabel-muench-51168b2/

Cindy Murphy
@CindyMurph

President-Gillware Digital Forensics, Madison WI - 'The most pathetic person in the world is someone who has sight, but has no vision.' Helen Keller

Cindy Murphy is president at Gillware Digital Forensics, based in Madison, Wisconsin.

Cindy is a highly respected expert in the digital forensics field. Her career is rooted in law enforcement. She served as an MP for the U.S. Army, was a VA police officer, and worked as a sworn officer and detective for the Madison Police Department from 1991-2016.

She began investigating computer-related crimes in 1998 and earned her M.Sc. in Forensic Computing and Cybercrime Investigation from University College, Dublin, in 2011.

A proponent for developing future digital forensics investigators, Cindy has created coursework and taught for collegiate programs. She co-authored and taught the SANS FOR585 Advanced Smartphone Forensics course.

Cindy's recognitions include 2016 Women of Influence in IT Security, SC Magazine; 2014 SANS People Who Made a Difference in Security Award; 2012 Forensic 4Cast Forensic Examiner of the Year Award; and SANS Lethal Forensicator Coin Recipient.

linkedin.com/in/detectivecindymurphy/

Lysa Myers
@LysaMyers

Security researcher, privacy connoisseur. Mini-farmer, weed-eater. Aposematic. She/ her

Lysa Myers is a security researcher at ESET, an IT security company that offers antivirus and firewall products.

She began her security career with McAfee Security. She was with the company for nine years and held a variety of roles, including senior virus research lead. She was also director of research at West Coast Labs and senior security analyst at Intego.

Lysa is an elected member of the CompTIA IT Security Council and currently serves as vice chair. She is a frequent contributor to a variety of security magazines, including We Live Security, Dark Reading, and CSOonline. She is a frequent speaker at events including (ISC)2 Security Congress, CompTIA ChannelCon, Virus Bulletin, AVAR, and Xconomy Forum.

She is dedicated to improving diversity within the technology industry, both as a way to decrease the skills gap and to make secure devices and applications that are useful for a larger segment of the population.

In her free time, Lysa runs a mini farm and food forest with her spouse. Their farm specializes in miniature livestock animals, as well as traditional native Pacific Northwest food plants.

linkedin.com/in/lysamyers/

Wendy Nather
@wendynather

Head of Advisory CISOs at @duosec (now @Cisco). Recovering industry analyst, research director and CISO. My opinions, let me show you them.

Wendy Nather has more than 30 years of experience in IT operations and security, including twelve years in the financial services industry and five years in state government. She is presently head of Advisory CISOs at Duo Security, recently acquired by Cisco. She leads a team of CISO strategists that engage both internally and externally to build on a new vision for information security.

Previously, Wendy was the research director at the Retail Cyber Intelligence Sharing Center (R-CISC) and for 451 Research's Information Security Practice. She led IT security for the EMEA region of the investment banking division of Swiss Bank Corporation and served as Texas Education Agency's CISO.

She speaks regularly on topics ranging from threat intelligence to identity and access management, risk analysis, incident response, data security, and societal and privacy issues.

Wendy co-authored "The Cloud Security Rules: Technology is your Friend. And Enemy." The book, which explains the different aspects of cloud security, was written by some of the most recognized security specialists and bloggers in the world.

Wendy was listed as one of SC Magazine's Women in IT Security "Power Players" in 2014.

linkedin.com/in/wendynather/

Dr. Angela Orebaugh
@angelaorebaugh

Professor @UVA, teaching the 21st century workforce | Futurist | Cybersecurity | Sustainability Evangelist | Author | Speaker | Philanthropist | Adventurer

Angela Orebaugh, Ph.D. is a technology futurist and thought leader who synergizes her 20 years of strategic and technical experience within commercial, academic, and government environments to advise clients on next-generation technologies and disruptive innovation. She evangelizes the impact of smart technology by highlighting the powerful ways in which these technologies are changing business, communications, and information sharing.

Dr. Orebaugh is an internationally recognized author of best-selling technology books including "Wireshark and Ethereal Network Protocol Analyzer Toolkit," "Ethereal Packet Sniffing," and "Nmap in the Enterprise." She co-authored the "Snort Cookbook," "Intrusion Prevention and Active Response," and "How to Cheat at Configuring Open Source Security Tools."

She is an invited speaker at a variety of conferences and technology events. She was the 2013 recipient of Information Security Magazine's Security 7 Award and one of the 2011 Femmonomics Top 50 Women in Tech to Watch. She was named Booz Allen Hamilton's first Cybersecurity Fellow in 2011.

linkedin.com/in/angelaorebaugh/

Theresa Payton
@TrackerPayton

CEO @FortaliceLLC | Cybersecurity & Intelligence Specialists | TV @HuntedCBS Team | Speaker - @KepplerSpeakers | Passionate protector for companies & people

Theresa Payton is one of the nation's leading experts in cybersecurity and IT strategy. She is the CEO of Fortalice Solutions, an industry-leading security consulting company, and co-founder of Dark Cubed, a cybersecurity product company. Theresa also starred in the CBS show, "Hunted."

She began her career in financial services. Following executive roles with Bank of America and Wachovia, she served as the first female chief information officer at the White House, overseeing IT operations for President George W. Bush and his staff. In 2015, she was named a William J. Clinton distinguished lecturer by the Clinton School of Public Service.

Theresa is the author of several publications on IT strategy and cybersecurity and a frequent speaker on IT risk. In 2014, she co-authored "Privacy in the Age of Big Data: Recognizing Threats, Defending Your Rights, and Protecting Your Family."

She has been named one of the top 25 Most Influential People in Security by Security Magazine and One of Infosec's Rising Stars and Hidden Gems by Tripwire.

linkedin.com/in/theresapayton/

Nicole Perlroth

@nicoleperlroth

spies on spies spying on spies' spying | cybersecurity reporter @nytimes | it'd be tragic if those evil robots win | open dm | msg me for signal

Nicole Perlroth has been a reporter with The New York Times for seven years and covers cybersecurity.

Nicole is the recipient of several journalism awards for her reporting on efforts by the Chinese government to steal military and industrial trade secrets. She was awarded Winner, Best Technology Coverage, by the Society of American Business Editors and Writers and was selected as one of the Top Cybersecurity Journalists by the SANS Institute in 2014.

Her Times profile of security blogger Brian Krebs ("Reporting from the Web's Underbelly") was optioned by Sony Pictures.

Prior to joining the The New York Times in 2011, she was deputy editor at Forbes Magazine and covered venture capital and startups.

Nicole is currently at work on a cybersecurity book on the underground cyberweapons market titled "This Is How They Tell Me The World Ends" for Penguin/Portfolio.

Nicole is a guest lecturer at the Stanford Graduate School of Business. She is a graduate of Princeton University (B.A.) and Stanford University (M.A.).

linkedin.com/in/nicoleperlroth/

Quiessence Phillips
@itsquiessence

Polished exterior, Techie interior | InfoSec Unicorn | Creator of @securingurpath | Cofounder @ourjourni | At the intersection of NYC and Cybersecurity

Quiessence Phillips is deputy CISO and head of Threat Management, City of New York. She leads efforts for the SOC, CERT and Cyber Threat Intelligence (CTI) functions, which are part of the newly formed New York City Cyber Command.

Previously, she was VP, Cyber Security Operations - Incident Response, at Barclays. She was senior information security analyst at LookingGlass Cyber Solutions and served as information security analyst and then operations supervisor, National Incident Response Team, Federal Reserve Bank of New York.

She is the co-founder of JOURNi, an organization dedicated to equipping urban communities with the skills and resources necessary to jump-start their local economies. Their goal is to build an authentically inclusive tech ecosystem in the city of Detroit, by tapping into the heart and spirit of its residents. They provide immersive courses, youth-centered programming, beneficial employment opportunities, startup education, and socioeconomic resources.

Quiessence also created "Securing Your Path," a community for women interested in forging their path in the security industry.

linkedin.com/in/quiessencephillips/

Becky Pinkard
@BeckyPinkard

Cyber security executive, published author and proessional speaker. I do security because I love it. 2016 Security Champion of the Year, Women in IT Awards

Becky Pinkard is an information security executive, speaker, and published author. She is VP, IT and Intelligence at Digital Shadows, a SaaS-based security company that monitors, manages and remediates digital risk across the widest range of data sources within the open, deep, and dark web.

She is also the co-founder of Women Empowering Diversity in Startups (WEDS), a network founded by women in startups who believe that diversity and inclusion of all kinds are essential and drive happiness and success in the workplace.

Becky has two decades of experience in the security field. She was the director of Pearson's Security Operations Center. She served as global manager of BlackBerry's Security Operations Centre and as global head, Attack and Data Leakage Monitoring, Barclays Bank. She also held security positions with Verizon, PepsiCo, Harley Davidson Financial Services, and Cingular Wireless. She was a certified instructor with the SANS Institute for 14 years.

Becky was named 2016 Security Champion of the Year, Women in IT, Cybersecurity Excellence Awards.

linkedin.com/in/bpinkard/

Kymberlee Price
@Kym_Possible

Manager of Microsoft Security Response Center Community Programs Team +++ I don't tweet often +++ My opinions are mine, get your own

Vulnerability disclosure maven Kymber-lee Price has 15 years of experience in the information security industry, specializing in application security incident response and investigations. She currently leads the Micro-soft Security Response Center's Community Programs team as principal security PM manager. She pioneered the first security researcher outreach program in the software industry at Microsoft in 2003 and was initially with the company for more than nine years.

She was a principal investigator in the Zotob criminal investigation and analyzed APT's at Microsoft.

Kymberlee was the first incident manager hired into BlackBerry Security. She served as director of Synack's Red Team Strategic Oper-ations and later directed the efforts of crowd-sourced penetration testers at Bugcrowd as senior director of researcher operations. She returned to Microsoft in 2017.

She speaks regularly on vulnerability management and product incident response best practices at conferences around the world including Kaspersky Security Analyst Summit, Black Hat, RSA, Nullcon, and Metricon.

She holds dual Bachelor of Science degrees in behavioral psychology and public health education.

linkedin.com/in/kymberleeprice/

Tiffany Strauchs Rad
@TiffanyRad

Computer security researcher, professor, and lawyer. My comments are my own.

Tiffany Strauchs Rad is CEO and co-founder of Anatrope, Inc., which develops wireless automotive technologies for the security and data analytics industries. Her independent research was listed as #4 in "Top 10 White Hat Hacks" by Bloomberg and she is a contributor to the book, "Security in 2020."

She was also featured in 2013 in the Discovery Channel's documentary, "The Real Story: Live Free or Die Hard," based on the movie "Live Free or Die Hard." Her research was featured on the USA series, "Mr. Robot," in the season one episode titled "Brave Traveler."

Tiffany is an adjunct professor at the University of Southern Maine. She teaches computer security, law and ethics, in the computer science department.

Previously, she was manager of Operational Security, Embedded Technologies, at Cisco. She served as manager of Threat Research, ThreatGRID (now a Cisco company). She was part of GReAT (Global Research and Analysis Team), Kaspersky Lab.

Tiffany also served as an attorney and cyersecurity engineer for Battelle.

linkedin.com/in/
tiffany-strauchs-rad-3268962/

Roselle Safran
@RoselleSafran

#Mother, #entrepreneur, #cybersecurity specialist; into #worldtravel and #sustainability

Roselle Safran is the entrepreneur in residence at Lytical Ventures, a venture capital firm that invests in early-stage cybersecurity companies. She is also president of Rosint Labs, a consultancy to security teams, leaders, and startups.

Roselle is a frequent speaker on cybersecurity and entrepreneurship for conferences, corporate events, webinars, and podcasts. She was the co-founder and CEO of Uplevel Security, which garnered numerous industry accolades under her leadership.

Previously, Roselle managed cybersecurity operations at the Executive Office of the President during the Obama Administration, directing the tactical, operational, and strategic work of the Security Operations Center that protected and defended the White House's network.

Before that, she managed analysis teams at the Department of Homeland Security's US-CERT and spearheaded the development of two cyber-threat intelligence platforms there.

Roselle holds a certified information systems security professional (CISSP) certification and a Bachelor of Science in engineering from Princeton University.

linkedin.com/in/rosellesafran/

Dr. Phyllis A. Schneck
@PromontoryFG

Former Deputy Undersecretary for Cybersecurity and Communications, U.S. Department of Homeland Security.

Dr. Phyllis Schneck has 15+ years of government and private-sector experience in senior cybersecurity positions. In her role as managing director and global leader of Promontory Cyber Solutions, she heads the worldwide cybersecurity practice. She has a background in high-performance computing and its applications to cyber threat intelligence and cryptography. She joined Promontory from the Department of Homeland Security. She served as the deputy undersecretary for cybersecurity and communications and led responses to cybersecurity threats against corporations, civilians, and the government. Prior to the DHS, Phyllis served as CTO, global public sector, at McAfee.

She was a member of the Center for Strategic and International Studies' commission that advised President Obama on cybersecurity and chairman of the board of directors of the National Cyber-Forensics and Training Alliance. She was vice chairman of the National Institute of Standards and Technology's advisory board on information security and privacy and national chairman of the board of directors of the FBI's InfraGard program for eight years. She has briefed and worked with several foreign governments to form partnerships with the U.S. for information sharing, infrastructure protection, and cybersecurity. She holds several information-security and technology patents.

promontory.com/bios.aspx?id=4491

Stephanie Scheuermann
@stephsscheuer

Cyber Threat Intelligence Specialist at Ford Motor Company

Stephanie Scheuermann has been with Ford Motor Company for 19 years. She began her current position as a cyber threat intelligence specialist in 2014. In this position, she has defined the vision and spearheaded the initiation of a cyber-threat intelligence capability for the enterprise.

She was tasked with defining the strategy and gaining support across the organization to deliver an effective cyber-threat intelligence capability that includes actively defending through disciplined, analyst and intelligence driven security.

In her role as computer incident response supervisor (CIRT), she developed concept and obtained funding for a cybersecurity program designed to grow the Ford capability to detect and respond to targeted cyber threats. This program laid the foundation for continued growth and sustainable investment in people, processes and technology in recognition of a dynamic threat landscape. This included creation of organizational structure and technical career opportunities globally.

She also served as CIRT and EDiscovery Forensic Services supervisor.

linkedin.com/in/
stephanie-scheuermann-2494408/

Amber Schroader
@gingerwondermom

I like to keep it simple. I am a Mom. I am a Digital Forensic Geek. I am a ginger. I am fighting for awareness to digital problems with devices and data.

Amber Schroader is the founder of Paraben Corporation and serves as president and CEO as well as the chief architect responsible for the design of Paraben's extensive line of digital forensic solutions.

Throughout the past two decades, Amber has been a driving force for innovation in digital forensics. She has developed over two dozen software programs designed to recover digital data from hand-held devices such as cellular phones and PDAs, computer hard drives, and large-scale computer networks capable of storing data from several thousand computers.

With an aggressive development schedule, she continues to bring forth new and exciting technology to the computer forensic community worldwide. She coined the concept of the "360-degree approach to digital forensics," pushing for a big-picture consideration of the digital evidence acquisition process.

An accomplished curriculum developer and instructor, Amber has written and taught numerous classes for this specialized field. She continues support through book contributions and other industry speaking engagements.

linkedin.com/in/amberschroader/

Masha Sedova
@modMasha

Transforming security behaviors from have to to want to through behavioral science. Co-founder of @hello_Elevate

Masha Sedova is an industry-recognized people-security expert, speaker, and trainer focused on engaging people to be key elements of secure organizations. She is the co-founder of Elevate Security, an innovative approach to security awareness.

Elevate's Security Behavior Platform leverages the latest advances in behavioral and data science delivered through innovative training, reward and feedback experiences, and decades of expertise in elevating employee behaviors. Elevate motivates and empowers employees to do the right thing while giving security teams comprehensive visibility and insight into the status and improvement of the organizations' employee-centered security posture and performance.

Before Elevate, Masha was a security executive at Salesforce where she built and led the security engagement team focused on improving the security mindset of employees, partners, and customers. Previously, she was a member of the board of directors for the National Cyber Security Alliance.

She is a regular presenter at conferences such as Black Hat, RSA, ISSA, Enigma, and SANS.

linkedin.com/in/msedova/

Rinki Sethi
@rinkisethi

Woman in Tech and Cyber, Mom, @Warriors fan, VP & CISO @Rubrik, Former leader @Intuit, @eBay, @Walmart @PaloAltoNtwks @IBM

Rinki Sethi has developed and implemented innovative security infrastructure for Fortune 500 companies including IBM, Palo Alto Networks, Walmart.com, Intuit, and eBay.

She has more than 15 years of experience leading strategy and vision in product security, security operations, and security architecture. She recently transitioned from her role as VP, Information Security for IBM to Rubrik, where she serves as VP and CISO.

While with IBM, Rinki led a team of more than 500 and was responsible for building an internal center of excellence for IBM's security functions, a world-class security operations center, and an identity and access management practice.

Her accomplishments include building a $10 million security infrastructure for Walmart.com and a $7 million mini-NASA mission control center that intercepts anywhere from 100 million to billions of attacks for Palo Alto Networks. She established security strategies for eBay's 30+ adjacent businesses.

Rinki serves on the board of directors of Women in CyberSecurity (WiCyS). She is an Everwise mentor and a member of ISACA, (ISC)2, SANS, IEEE, and InfraGard.

linkedin.com/in/rinkisethi/

Dr. Ambareen Siraj
@ambareensiraj

Professor, Computer Science, Tennessee Tech, Founder WiCyS

Dr. Ambareen Siraj is the founder and conference chair of Women in CyberSecurity (WiCyS), a community of engagement, encouragement, and support for women in cybersecurity. WiCys is dedicated to bringing together women in cybersecurity from academia, research, and industry to share knowledge, experience, networking, and mentoring.

Dr. Siraj is the founding director of Tennessee Tech's Cybersecurity Education, Research and Outreach Center (CEROC) and a professor in the Computer Science department. She is the program director of NSF CyberCorps, DoD CySP, and NSA-NSF GenCyber Camp at Tennessee Tech.

She leads several National Science Foundation projects. Her effort to educate students and enhance the cybersecurity field of study goes beyond classes, research and outreach projects, workshops and conferences. She has authored or co-authored more than 40 journal and conference articles while taking an active part in promoting cybersecurity training throughout the nation.

Dr. Siraj is a frequent speaker in various cybersecurity conferences nationwide. She is the recipient of the Colloquium for Information Systems Security Education Exceptional Leadership in Education Award in 2018.

linkedin.com/in/ambareensiraj/

Reeny Sondhi
@reenysondhi

Chief Security Officer @Autodesk; passionate supporter of #diversityintech; Views my own

Reeny Sondhi is a senior technology and cloud security executive who has worked successfully in startups and larger corporations. She has spent the last 14+ years building transformational enterprise scale security programs.

She is currently vice president and chief security officer at Autodesk. She is responsible for driving all security related strategy and decisions across the company and leads the teams responsible for the security of infrastructure, cloud, products and services, as well as the teams dedicated to security governance, risk and compliance, and security incident response.

Previously, Reeny was senior director of Security Engineering & Assurance, EMC. She has many years of product management experience, having conceptualized, created, and brought multiple software and hardware products to market.

She is passionate about promoting diversity in technology and information security. She serves as a mentor for the Autodesk Women in Technology program and is a sponsor for the Emerging Leaders Program.

Reeny holds a Bachelor of Science in electronics & telecommunications and a Master of Business Administration.

linkedin.com/in/reenysondhi/

Myrna Soto
@Myrna_Soto

Venture Capital Partner - Former SVP & Global CISO, Corp Board Member, Golfer, Human Rights Advocate, Foodie, & Wine Enthusiast Tweets here are my own.

Myrna Soto is currently chief operating officer at Digital Hands, a managed security services provider. She has responsibility for security operations, sales, marketing, human resources, and customer success.

Myrna is also on the board of directors of Spirit Airlines and Consumers Energy and is an advisory board member of Bay Dynamics and strategic advisor to the CEO.

Recently, she was a partner at ForgePoint Capital, focusing on cybersecurity investments. She served as corporate SVP and global CISO for Comcast Corporation, a telecommunications and media conglomerate, for more than nine years.

She has more than 26 years of technology leadership experience in multiple operational roles across varied industries, including American Express, Royal Caribbean Cruise Lines, Kemper Insurance, and MGM Resorts.

Myrna was recognized as one of the World's Top IT Security Influencers by CISO Platform in 2018 and Fortune's 50 Most Powerful Latinas in Business in 2018 and 2017. SC Magazine has included her in its top 10 Power Players for Women in Security. She was named in the top 100 Technology Executives by the Hispanic IT Executive Council.

linkedin.com/in/myrnasoto/

Suzanne Spaulding
@SpauldingSez

Former DHS Under Secretary for cyber and infrastructure protection. Senior Advisor for Homeland Security and International Security Program at CSIS

Suzanne Spaulding is senior advisor for the Center for Strategic and International Studies (CSIS). She spent nearly 30 years working national security issues in the private sector, the executive branch, and Congress. She served as undersecretary for the National Protection and Programs Directorate at the Department of Homeland Security (DHS), where she was effectively the CEO, with a rank equivalent to a four-star general.

She managed a $3 billion budget and a workforce of more than 18,000 Feds and contractors charged with strengthening cybersecurity and protecting the nation's critical infrastructure. She led the transformation of budget, acquisition, analytic, and operational processes to bring greater agility and unity of effort to an organization that had experienced dramatic growth through acquisition of new entities and missions over several years.

Suzanne has advised CEOs, boards, and government policymakers on how to manage complex security risks. She has convened and participated in numerous academic and professional advisory panels, been a frequent commentator in public media, and has often testified before Congress.

linkedin.com/in/
suzanne-spaulding-9a90a5137/

Jennifer Sunshine Steffens
@securesun

Living and loving the pirate life at IOActive - a global security research and services firm

Jennifer Sunshine Steffens is CEO at IOActive. She spearheads all aspects of the company's global business operations and drives its strategic vision.

Jennifer is recognized as one of the top leaders in information security. She is an active member of the Executive Women's Forum, the Information Systems Security Association (ISSA), and the Open Web Application Security Project.

Lauded by Forbes, The Wall Street Journal, Information Security Magazine, and many more, she received SC Magazine's Reboot Leadership Award for Top Management in 2017 and CV Magazine's IT Security CEO of the Year 2018.

She is a judge for the Tech Trailblazers and DUO Women in Security awards and a frequent speaker at events around the world. Prior to joining IOActive, she came to Seattle to help startup GraniteEdge reinvent itself. She led initiatives to restructure the company and developed a product strategy that ultimately led to a successful acquisition.

Jennifer has held leadership positions at groundbreaking companies such as Sourcefire and NFR Security. She is an advisory board member of the London Office for Rapid Cybersecurity Advancement (LORCA).

linkedin.com/in/jsteffens/

Dr. Chanel Suggs
@duchess_cysec

Professor #Cybersecurity, #Hacker, #AI, #Cryptography, #Forensics, Entrepreneur, Cyber Advisor, #Speaker,#Women Empowerment. Hacking with a purpose.

Dr. Chanel Suggs — Duchess of Cybersecurity ® — is the CEO and founder of Wyvern Security. She works with clients to uncover and identify new and emerging threats and defend against attacks.

She is a proven thought leader and a subject matter expert in cybersecurity, cryptography, forensics, network security, computing, information assurance, and IT strategy. She is also a distinguished lecturer. As a keynote speaker, her methods of assessing the hacker methodology provide ways to view attacks through the eyes of a hacker. Dr. Suggs asserts that "adapting to the hacker mindset will enable you to create proactive measures."

She was awarded six certifications through the National Security Agency (NSA). She holds 19 certifications within the InfoSec, forensics and cybersecurity community.

She has been featured in EXPOSED! Cyber-Security Handbook, The Washington Post, EC-Council, the Miami Herald, and Yahoo! Finance. She has appeared on CNN, CBS, ABC, Fox, and NBC, as well as various radio shows and podcasts.

Dr. Suggs promotes women and diversity in cybersecurity. She focuses on rural community outreach and fundraising for these initiatives.

linkedin.com/in/chanelsuggs/

Parisa Tabriz
@laparisa

Browser Boss @googlechrome; Security Princess @google; Project Zero den mom; former @usds; skilled at baking, eating, and hijacking cookies.

Parisa Tabriz is an engineering leader that likes to help teams solve important problems at the intersection of information, technology, and humanity. She has been with Google since 2007 and is presently browser boss (senior engineering director), House of Chrome.

She previously held the title of security princess (security engineering manager, information security engineering manager, and software engineer). She is responsible for the Chrome browser shipped on Windows, Mac, Linux, and Chrome OS, plus lots of features that make Chrome useful across desktop and mobile (e.g. sync, autofill, password management, and more). She also manages Project Zero, an offensive security research team that aims to make 0-day hard.

Between November 2014 and November 2016, Parisa was a consultant to the United States Digital Service. She advised the Executive Office of the President on industry best practices to enhance network and software security.

In March 2015, she worked with members of the Defense Digital Service to help assess status of the OCX project, dubbed "the most troubled program," from the U.S. Air Force.

linkedin.com/in/parisa-tabriz-a676472/

Sandra Toms

@sandra001

Cyber security geek. Creates experiences that bring people together to discuss important technology, topics and policy @RSAConference.

Recognized as a 2017 Top 50 Women in Cybersecurity, Sandra Toms has served as VP and curator, RSA Conference, since 1998. She grew the conference into the world's largest cybersecurity industry event and a globally recognized brand in security. She increased global attendance from under 2,000 to nearly 50,000 by creating an external selection committee to select talks from a fiercely competitive speaking submission process.

Sandra collaborates with Fortune 500 cybersecurity C-Suite executives, including 15 distinguished experts serving with her on the RSA Conference Advisory Board, to bring the best of the industry together each year. She is passionate about bringing the security industry together, empowering the collective "we" of the industry to stand against cyber threats around the world, and introducing new programming and facilitating conversations that tackle key industry challenges like the skills gap, talent shortage, and diversity.

Sandra holds a B.A. in psychology from UCLA and a J.D. from Santa Clara University, where she graduated cum laude and was the managing editor of the High Tech Law Journal.

linkedin.com/in/sandra-toms-419277/

Verónica Valeros Saracho
@verovaleros

Woman. Hacker. Mentor. Speaker. Malware Researcher. Studying Remote Access Trojans. Working at @civilsphere / Founder @womenintechfund & @mateslab

Verónica Valeros Saracho is a hacker and researcher from Argentina. Her research has a strong focus on helping people and involves different areas, from wireless and bluetooth privacy issues to malware, botnets, and intrusion analysis. She has presented her research at international conferences such as Black Hat, EkoParty, Botconf, Troopers, and others.

Verónica is the co-founder of the MatesLab hackerspace based in Argentina and of the Independent Fund for Women in Tech, which aims to change the participation ratio of women at security conferences by providing free tickets to those events. She is part of the core team of Security Without Borders, a collective of cybersecurity professionals who volunteer assisting people at risk and NGOs on cybersecurity issues.

Previously, she was a software engineer at Cisco. From 2013 to early 2018, she worked in the Cognitive Threat Analytics team, specializing in malware network traffic analysis and threat hunting at big scale. She joined the Czech Technical University in Prague in 2018 and leads the CivilSphere project.

In her spare time, she studies and researches remote access trojans in a project called A Study of RATs.

linkedin.com/in/veronicavalerossaracho/

Georgia Weidman
@georgiaweidman

Author: Penetration Testing nostarch.com/pentesting Founder: @bulbsecurity & @shevirahsec Professor: @UMUC & @tulane Fellow: @NewAmerica

Georgia Weidman is a serial entrepreneur, penetration tester, security researcher, speaker, trainer, mentor, and author. Her work in smartphone exploitation received a DARPA Cyber Fast Track grant and has been featured internationally in print and on television. Georgia is the author of "Penetration Testing: A Hands-On Introduction to Hacking." She has presented or conducted training around the world including Black Hat, DEF CON, NSA, and West Point.

Georgia founded Shevirah to create products for assessing and managing the risk of mobile devices in the enterprise and testing the effectiveness of enterprise mobility management solutions. She is also the founder of the security consulting firm Bulb Security. She is a graduate of and a mentor at the MACH37 Cyber Accelerator and an angel investor.

Georgia received the 2015 Women's Society of Cyberjutsu Pentest Ninja award. She is on the board of advisors at the cybersecurity training startup Cybrary, an adjunct professor at Tulane University and University of Maryland University College, a member of the CyberWatch Center's National Visiting Committee, and a Cybersecurity Policy Fellow at New America.

linkedin.com/in/georgiaweidman/

Christy Wheaton
@christy_wheaton

CISO, Information Technology Executive, Information Security Specialist
Professional account for managing news feeds, topics of interest and relationships.

Christy Wheaton is vice president and chief information privacy and security officer (CIPSO), CISSP and C|CISO at Henry Ford Health System. She previously served as the senior director and CISO for Meritor, overseeing the enterprise cybersecurity and GRC programs globally.

Prior to that, she served as global identity and access management lead for GE Capital, overseeing global IAM programs. Her role expanded to overseeing the information security intelligence program, and information security risk, governance, and compliance programs.

Earlier in her career, she rotated through the director and CIO roles for Ally Bank, holding several roles in motors insurance, corporate security, and global sales and service management. She oversaw various IT departments and IT and infosec, data protection, governance, risk and compliance programs.

She is a 2018 Stevie Silver Winner, American Business Awards.

linkedin.com/in/chrisywheaton/

Wendi Whitmore

@wendiwhitmore

Global Lead IBM X-Force IRIS, Formerly CrowdStrike & Mandiant. All views are my own.

Wendi Whitmore has more than 16 years of diverse experience in the incident response and threat intelligence services industry. She is global partner and director of IBM X-Force Threat Intelligence and global partner and lead of IBM X-Force Incident Response & Intelligence Services (IRIS). She created the IRIS team in 2016. She and her team grew it from inception to a Forrester Quadrant One incident response leader in less than three years.

Wendi frequently speaks to executive boards and at a variety of high-profile technical conferences. She has been a featured speaker at Black Hat, RSA, SANS, the Fortune Most Powerful Women Summit, and the WSJ Academy, among others. She has been a keynote speaker at Cyber Tech and the Women in CyberSecurity (WiCyS) conference. She has instructed graduate level computer science and cybersecurity courses at Carnegie Mellon and George Washington University and has been profiled in Fast Company, Dark Reading, and SC Magazine.

Prior to IBM, Wendi held executive leadership roles within the consulting organizations at CrowdStrike and Mandiant / FireEye. Before Mandiant, she was a special agent conducting computer crime investigations with the Air Force Office of Special Investigations (AFOSI).

linkedin.com/in/wendiwhitmore2/

Laura Whitt-Winyard
@L_WhittWinyard

Global Chief Information Security Officer Opinions are my own. Nerd. DEFCON regular. Cubs fan. Security evangelist.

Laura Whitt-Winyard, CISSP, CISM, CISA, CRISC, is the global CISO of DLL, leading the information security program in 30+ countries. She is a security evangelist and visionary leader in the areas of information security, privacy, compliance, and risk management.

She has 18 years of information security experience, including leading highly effective and successful information security programs, products, and services. She served as the director of information security at Billtrust, where she was responsible for establishing and maintaining a corporate-wide information security management program.

Previously, she held roles as the senior manager of information security at Comcast, and at Bloomberg for several years prior, she was global head of Security Oversight.

She was an ISE Executive of the Year nominee. Under her leadership, her teams have been nominated for many security industry awards, such as ISE National Project Finalists, RSA Archer Innovation Awards and CSO40/50 Awards.

linkedin.com/in/laurawhittwinyard/

Elisabetta Zaccaria
@ElZaccaria

#cybersecurity #tech #founder @ cyberYLondon, #Chairman @ SecureChorus, former #COO #CSO Global Strategies Group (from UK start-up to global biz $600M in 6 years)

Elisabetta Zaccaria is a C-level executive and entrepreneur with more than 15 years of experience in the cybersecurity sector internationally. She serves as chairman of Secure Chorus Ltd, a global platform for public-private sector cooperation in the development of resilient cyber ecosystems of technologies that are interoperable and secure by design.

Prior to that she was group chief strategy officer and chief operating officer of Global Strategies Group, a company operating at the technological cutting edge of defense and national security in the U.S. and globally. She played a key leadership role leading to the company's explosive growth, including several acquisitions, an IPO (Nasdaq) and an exit to a private equity house, turning the startup into a $600 million revenue international business in six years.

She has also served as board director of several technology companies. She is an entrepreneur mentor in residence at London Business School, a keynote speaker at major conferences, and an author and contributing writer to international information technology and business publications.

linkedin.com/in/elisabetta-z-2a016643/

Zeina Zakhour
@ZeinaZakhour

CyberSecurity Nut, CTO @Atos, #AtosSC member, #Journey2022 contributor, Business Strategy Enthusiast, lousy musician ... A melting pot Human. Tweets are my own

Zeina Zakhour has 17 years of experience in the cybersecurity field. She is the global CTO for Cybersecurity at Atos, creating innovative solutions to be a step ahead of cybercriminals.

She covers the end-to-end spectrum of cybersecurity from security advisory to security integration, managed security services, and IoT and big data security. She works closely with Fortune 500 companies to advise them regarding security strategy and help them secure their infrastructure and protect their data.

Zeina is a member of the Atos Scientific Community and a distinguished expert in cybersecurity. She is also a certified information systems security professional (CISSP) and a certified ISO 27005 risk manager.

Zeina has been with Atos for 15 years. Previously, she was a network and security consultant for Schlumberger and involved in infosec risk management at Orange.

She holds a Bachelor of Engineering in C.C.E from Notre Dame University Lebanon, an M. Sc. from Telecom Sud Paris, and an Executive MBA from HEC.

linkedin.com/in/zeinazakhour/

Kim Zetter
@KimZetter

**Journalist - cybersecurity/national security.
Author of COUNTDOWN TO ZERO DAY:
Stuxnet and the Launch of the World's
First Digital Weapon. Speaker. Signal user**

Kim Zetter is an award-winning investigative journalist who has covered cybersecurity, national security, surveillance, and the hacking underground since 1999, first for PC World magazine and then for WIRED, where she wrote for more than a decade.

More recently, she has been writing for The New York Times Magazine, Politico, The Washington Post, Motherboard, and others. She has four times been voted one of the top 10 security journalists in the U.S. by her journalism peers. She has broken numerous stories over the years about NSA surveillance and the agency's offensive hacking operations, WikiLeaks, and the hacker and cybercriminal undergrounds.

She has written extensively over the last 15 years about security problems with electronic voting machines and recently wrote a New York Times Magazine cover story on the topic called "The Crisis of Election Security."

She is considered a leading expert on Stuxnet, a groundbreaking virus/worm created by the U.S. and Israel to sabotage Iran's nuclear program. She wrote an acclaimed book on the topic, "Countdown to Zero Day: Stuxnet and the Launch of the World's First Digital Weapon."

linkedin.com/in/kim-zetter-20421b/

Index

D

E

F

H

I

J

O

T

V

W

Steve Morgan

 Steve Morgan is founder and editor-in-chief at Cybersecurity Ventures. He heads up all editorial and publishing at the world's leading independent researcher covering the global cyber economy, and a trusted source for cybersecurity facts, figures, predictions, and statistics.

Steve is also founder and editor-in-chief at Cybercrime Magazine, known as 'Page ONE for the Cybersecurity Industry' – featuring cyber economic data used by the world's largest media outlets, governments, academia, associations, vendors, and industry experts.

Over the past five years, Steve has authored more than 500 blogs, articles, and reports on cybersecurity and cybercrime for numerous media outlets including Forbes, CSO, Dark-Reading, Homeland Security Today, Entrepreneur, and Cybercrime Magazine.

Onalytica, an award-winning influencer marketing software platform, calculated Steve to be one of the "Top 100 Cybersecurity Influencers at RSA Conference USA 2019" (no. 67), where there were 42,000 attendees, 700 speakers, 650 exhibitions, 17 keynotes, and

550 sessions. LinkedIn named Steve in their "5 Security Influencers to Follow" in 2017. He's been named to numerous other cybersecurity lists over the past several years.

twitter.com/CybersecuritySF
linkedin.com/in/cybersecuritysf/
cybersecurityventures.com

Di Freeze

Di Freeze is managing editor at Cybercrime Magazine. She is responsible for posting and managing blogs, reports, lists, and community resources. She works closely with the editor-in-chief, writers, and contributors. She also manages research and compilation for special projects, including @WomenKnowCyber.

Previously, she was an editor at Sand Hill, a software industry blog and newsletter, for nearly five years.

Before that, Di was editor-in-chief at Airport Journals, a national aviation publication, for more than nine years. She oversaw writers, photographers, news editors, copy editors, and proofreaders. During that period, she interviewed many of the world's most well-known aviators, including miliary pilots, astronauts, entrepreneurs, record breakers, and Hollywood celebrities.

Di founded Freeze Time Media to publish those biographies in a print and digital book series, "Passion for Flight." She has helped dozens of new authors get their books in print.

twitter.com/difreeze
linkedin.com/in/difreeze/
freezetimemedia.com

Made in the USA
Middletown, DE
11 June 2019